HAMMOND UNDERCOVER™

HORSES

HAMMOND

Published in the United States and its territories and Canada by
HAMMOND WORLD ATLAS CORPORATION
part of the Langenscheidt Publishing Group

36-36 33rd Street, Long Island City, NY 11106

EXECUTIVE EDITOR: Nel Yomtov

ASSISTANT EDITOR: Kevin Somers

Produced for Hammond World Atlas Corporation by

MOSELEY ROAD INC.

129 MAIN STREET

IRVINGTON, NY 10533

WWW.MOSELEYROAD.COM

MOSELEY ROAD INC.

PUBLISHER Sean Moore

ART DIRECTORS Brian MacMullen, Gus Yoo

EDITORIAL DIRECTOR Lisa Purcell

EDITOR AMBER ROSE

PHOTO RESEARCHER Ben DeWalt

PRODUCTION DESIGNER Joanne Flynn

CARTOGRAPHY Neil Dvorak

EDITORIAL ASSISTANTS Rachael Lanicci, Natalie Rivera

COVER DESIGN Linda Kosarin

Printed and bound in Canada

ISBN-13: 978-0841-610941

HAMMOND UNDER C☉VER™

HORSES

FRAN HODGKINS

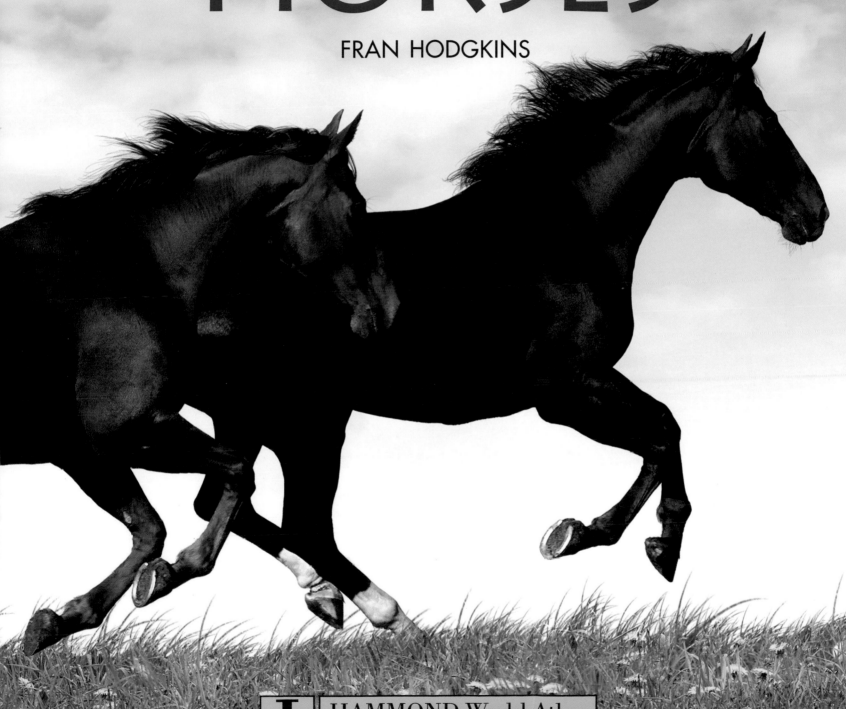

 HAMMOND World Atlas
Part of the Langenscheidt Publishing Group

Contents

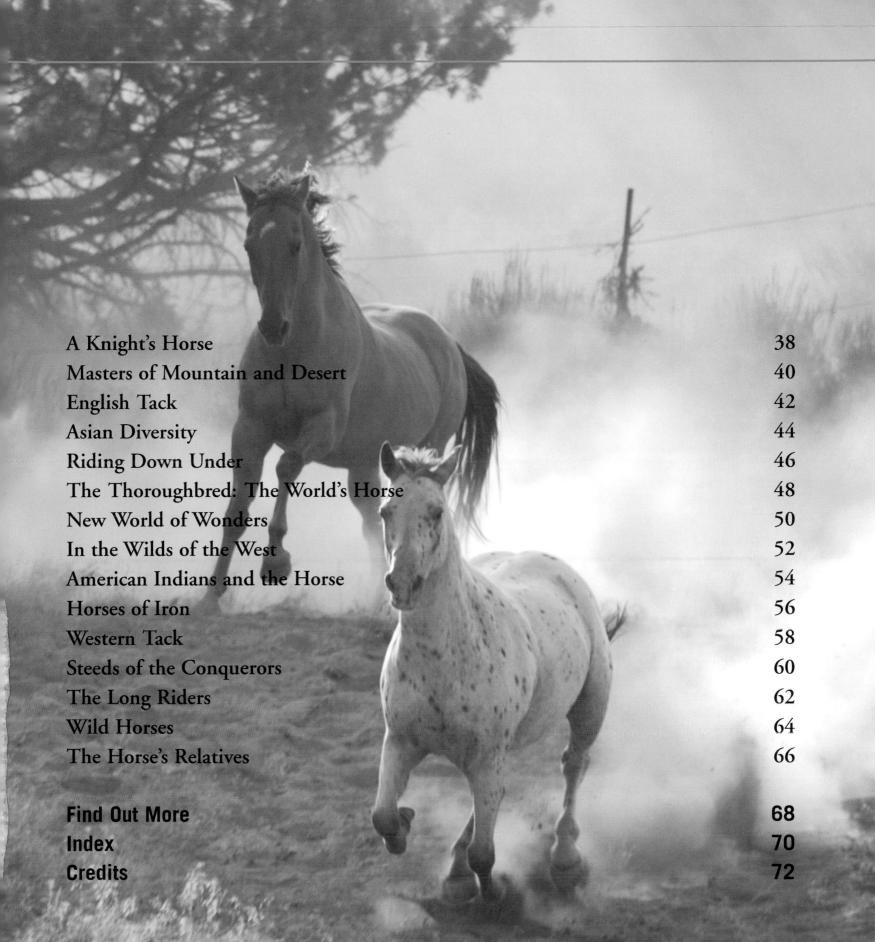

A Horse, of Course

If you could travel back in time, what animal would you see helping human beings the most?

The dog, perhaps. Well, the dog helped us hunt for food. And it could even carry stuff. But have you ever tried to ride a dog? All right, then: how about the cow? After all, the cow gives us food and milk. We use its hide for leather. And it could carry stuff, too. But have you ever tried to get anywhere fast with a cow? Aha, you might say. It must be the cat. Cats protect our stored grain from rats and mice. But honestly, have you ever seen anyone get a cat to do something it doesn't want to do?

Dogs, cows, and cats deserve a lot of credit. But for versatility, the horse beats other animals hands (or hoofs) down. The horse could not only carry stuff like the dog, but it could pull stuff a lot faster than the cow. The horse has been used for food, milk, hides, and hair over the years. And although horses aren't known for catching mice, they sure are a lot easier to train than cats!

You could even argue that the horse, not the dog, should be called man's best friend.

Horses are strong and pleasant workers—perfect help around the farm!

People enjoy horses not only because they're helpful partners and important to our history, but also because they can be beautiful, powerful, and loving companions.

Horses Through History

In this book, you'll find out more about the horse and how it has changed human life for the better around the world. Today, there are more than 150 distinct breeds of horse, from the tiny Falabella to the gigantic Shire. Some breeds have existed unchanged for thousands of years, while others have appeared only during the last few decades. Horse breeders are developing new breeds all the time.

Meanwhile, other, older breeds need protection: many are in danger of dying out.

Along the way, you'll learn some wild facts, such as why a horse can't vomit and what a quagga was. Here's hoping that you enjoy the ride!

Two Falabella miniature horses

Although humans rarely ride horses into war anymore, people still enjoy riding for pleasure or in competition with other riders.

Meet the Horse

You're driving along the highway with your family. You're bored. Suddenly, your brother shouts, "Hey, look! Horses!" Everybody in the car comes to life as they turn to watch a group of horses in a nearby field, grazing on grass, their coats shining in the sunlight.

Why don't people react the same way if the driver says, "Hey, cows!" or "Hey, corn!"? Both cows and corn are useful and important to our way of life. The horse has a mystique, a special something that sets it apart from the others. It's not just a farm animal. It's a part of our history and a part of our hearts. Even nonriders can admire and appreciate a beautiful horse.

In this section, you'll meet the horse. You'll find out what makes a horse a horse and what makes a pony a pony. You'll learn how horses evolved and about different horse types and breeds. And you'll discover some weird, wild, and even gross facts about horses, too.

Points of the Horse

The horse's body has its own geography. No matter how big or small a horse or pony is, every horse has the same parts, or points. It's the differences in the size and shape of the body's parts that make each breed distinct.

For example, the lower leg, or cannon bone, is shorter in some breeds than in others. Some horses, such as Shires, have convex or Roman face profiles. Other breeds have flat profiles, and the Arabian is famous for its dished, or concave, profile.

The Ideal Horse
Each established breed has a written description of the ideal member of that breed. This ideal description is called

DID YOU KNOW?

Horses have 205 bones in their bodies (humans have 206).

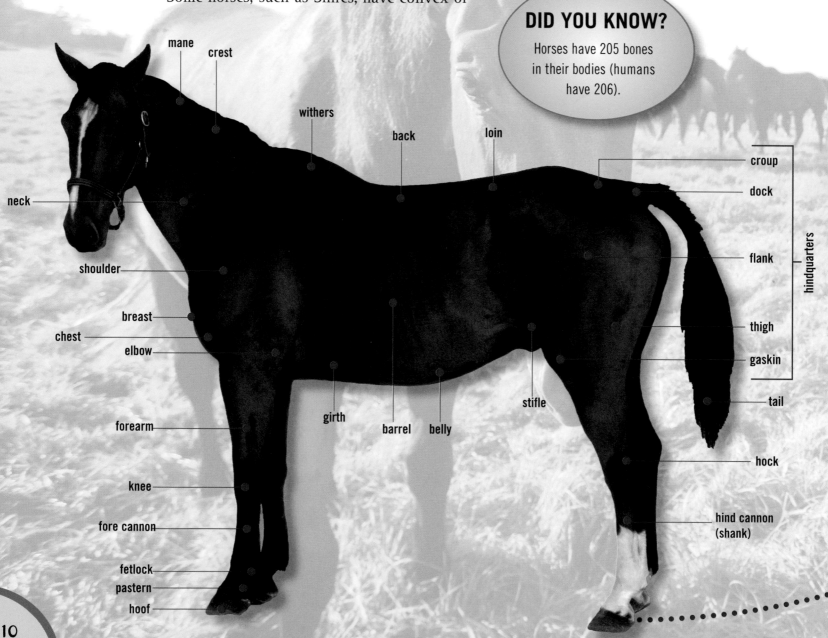

mane
crest
withers
back
loin
neck
croup
dock
shoulder
flank
hindquarters
breast
chest
thigh
elbow
gaskin
stifle
tail
girth
barrel belly
forearm
hock
knee
hind cannon
(shank)
fore cannon
fetlock
pastern
hoof

the breed standard. Horses that conform, or match, very closely to the breed's standard do well at horse shows where conformation is judged against the standard. Other horses that aren't quite up to the standard are still members of the breed and may make good pleasure mounts or work horses.

Cow Hocks and Knock Knees

Some individual horses have serious conformation problems. For example, if a horse's hocks point toward each other like a cow's, the horse is said to be cow-hocked. A horse whose knees push close together is knock-kneed, and if the front hooves point toward each other, the horse is pigeon-toed. Poor conformation limits a horse's ability to do certain activities, such as carry weight or run fast.

As you read the breed descriptions, you'll find certain points referred to often, such as the neck, withers, shoulder, and barrel. Flip back to this page if you aren't sure what the words mean.

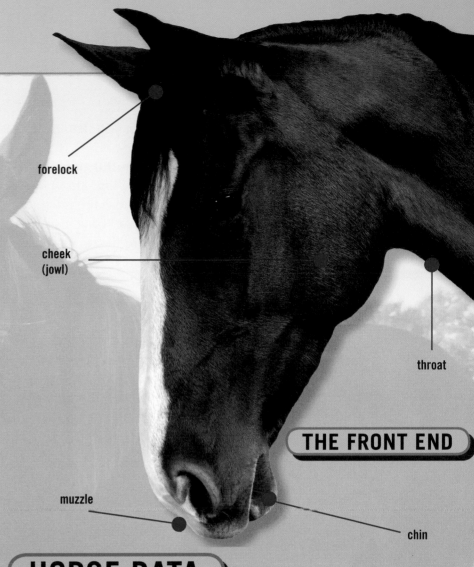

forelock

cheek (jowl)

throat

THE FRONT END

muzzle

chin

GOT A FROG IN YOUR . . . HORSE?!

EVERY HORSE comes with a frog. Four frogs, actually. No, they aren't in the horse's throat . . . they're part of the feet. The sole of a horse's foot is called the frog. It's softer than the rest of the hoof, which is hard and made of the same stuff as your fingernails.

HORSE DATA

HORSES ARE TRADITIONALLY measured in "hands." One hand equals four inches. So a 15-hand-high (hh) horse stands 60 inches tall at the withers, where the neck and back meet.

Don't let the decimal point fool you. A horse that is 15.1 hh is not actually 15 and one tenth of a hand tall. The .1 means "one inch," so the 15.1 hh horse is actually 61 inches tall (four inches times 15 equals 60, plus one equals 61). A 15.2 hh horse is 62 inches tall, and a 15.3 hh horse, 63 inches. How tall are you in hands? If you're four feet, you're 12 hh.

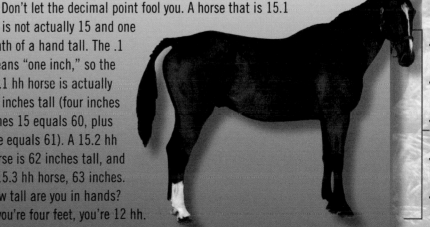

Creatures Great and Small

"A horse is a horse, of course, of course . . . " Or so the old song says. But there is no typical horse. They can be big, small, and everything in between, and have all sorts of personalities. Since it's important to know what kind of horse you're dealing with, people use many different terms to describe different types of horses.

Hot-Blooded

Some horses are called "hot-blooded." That doesn't mean that their blood is literally warmer than that of other horses. The term *hot-blooded* describes horses that are most famous for their speed and high-spirited temperaments. Hot-bloods include the Arabian and its descendants, especially the Thoroughbred.

Heavy Horses

Draft breeds, the "heavy horses" whose ancestors carried knights in the Middle Ages, are cold-blooded. Big and strong, these horses have easygoing temperaments—they keep their cool in most situations. That sure is a good thing, because a 2,000-pound, high-strung horse would be a disaster, hurting itself and the people around it if it spooked.

Not Too Hot, Not Too Cold

If you mix hot and cold, what do you get? Warm! That's exactly where warm-blooded horses, the other saddle horse breeds, come from. European cavalry soldiers needed horses with the speed of an Arabian or a Thoroughbred, but with gentler natures that could tolerate excitement and noise on the battlefield. By breeding these two horse types, they developed the warm-blooded breeds, such as the Irish hunter, the Hanoverian, the Trakehner, and the Selle Français (the French saddle horse). Originally from Europe, warm-bloods are finding enthusiastic homes and riders in the United States, too.

AVERAGE HORSE SIZES

Heavy horse
72 inches
18 hh

Warm- or Hot-blooded horse
60 inches
15 hh

SMALLER THAN A HORSE

WHAT'S A COB? A cob is larger than a pony but short for a horse (You'll read more about ponies later in this book). Cobs are powerfully built and short-legged. They look like smaller versions of their draft horse cousins.

Even smaller than cobs are miniature horses. Although small, they aren't ponies. In fact, these little guys are tiny for ponies! Some miniature foals stand just 1 foot tall—about the same as a house cat—and fully-grown miniature horses stand 34 inches tall, at the most.

What's the point in having such a little horse? Owners of mini horses say their little steeds are fun pets. Minis can also pull carts, jump fences, and do pretty much everything larger horses can do—except they can't be ridden by anyone who weighs more than 70 pounds. Minis are also working more and more often for disabled people. In fact, there are actually seeing-eye horses for blind people. Mares and geldings make good companions (stallions are often cranky with short fuses, but that's stallions for you).

So from the tiny miniature to the giant Shire, there's a horse of every size, for every need.

DID YOU KNOW?

What does "high-strung" or "high-spirited" mean? A horse's temperament (how it relates to people, other horses, and its surroundings) is incredibly important. A horse that reacts violently or unexpectedly to small things, like a piece of paper fluttering in the breeze, requires an experienced horse person. If you watch the Kentucky Derby on television, you'll see examples of high-spirited behavior when the handlers load the horses into the gate before the race!

Cob
58 inches
14.2 hh

Pony
44 inches
11 hh

Miniature horse
34 inches
8.2 hh

A Horse of a Different Color

Horses and ponies come in a rainbow of colors—well, not a rainbow exactly . . . no horse is pink or purple or anything silly like that. Horses do, however, show an amazing variety of colors and patterns.

COLORS AND PATTERNS

Colors and Markings

Although the first horses were a yellowish brown color called dun, today's horses come in everything from brilliant gold to black to a color called roan (roan horses look like they've been dusted with powdered sugar).

There are both coats of many colors and many patterns, too. Some horses have spotted hides, which can cover their entire bodies or just parts of them. One breed known for its spots is the Appaloosa. Others are splotched with white and another color. Called pintos or paints in the United States, these horses are called piebald (black and white) and skewbald (white and any color other than black) in Europe.

Many horses also have white markings on their faces and legs. Some breeds, like Clydesdales, may also have white marks on their bellies. These marks are called "flesh marks." To qualify for breed registration, however, white marks should be found only below the knee or hock. The white on the face should not go beyond the eyes, and there shouldn't be any white marks on the body.

DON'T GO THERE ON AN UGLY PLUG

"Plug ugly" means an ugly horse—*really* ugly. And don't ride an ugly plug in Hartsville, Illinois. It can get you arrested!

Spotted

Palomino

Bay

SPOTS, DOTS, AND BLONDS

DON'T CONFUSE a horse's color with its breed. Although some people may identify a horse as a "palomino," that's really just a color term, like "bay" or "chestnut."

A palomino is a golden horse with a white mane and tail. Many breeds can produce palomino horses. Buckskin horses have the same brown-gold body color as a palomino, but buckskins have black manes, tails, and lower legs.

A horse with spots may be an Appaloosa . . . or it may be something else. We know that spotted horses existed a long time before the Appaloosa became a breed.

The same thing goes for pintos. There are pinto-marked horses found in many breeds.

And to make matters more confusing, the horses of some breeds change color as they grow up. (Human hair sometimes does the same thing. For example, some brown-haired adults were blond-haired children.) So color may change, but breed remains!

Roan

HEAD MARKS

STAR
A small white mark on the center of the forehead

BLAZE
A wide white mark running the length of the face

STRIPE
A slender white mark running the length of the face

LEG MARKS

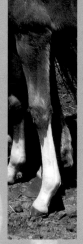

CORONET
A slim white band just above the hoof

PASTERN
A white band above the hoof

FETLOCK
A white band wide enough to just cover the fetlock

SOCK
White color extending above the fetlock and ending below the knee

STOCKING
White color covering the lower leg to the knee or higher

Horse vs. Pony

One of the most common questions about horses is, "Are horse and ponies different?" The answer is yes. And no.

Horses and ponies are members of the same species. A species is a group of animals or plants that can produce viable offspring (meaning that the offspring can reproduce, too). Both horses and ponies are scientifically classified as *Equus caballus*. (Other members of the *Equus* genus are zebras, donkeys, and asses—more on them later.)

HORSE BREEDS

Breed	Height
Arabian	14–15.3 hh
Caspian	10–12 hh
Galiceño	12–14 hh
Haflinger	13–15 hh
Kentucky Mountain saddle horse	11–15.2 hh
Morgan	14.1–15.2 hh
Peruvian Paso	14–15 hh
Sable Island	13–14 hh
Wilbur-Cruce Mission	14–15 hh

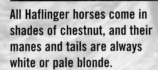

All Haflinger horses come in shades of chestnut, and their manes and tails are always white or pale blonde.

Peruvian Paso horses are named for their home country, Peru.

Short Horses and Tall Ponies

The technical difference between a horse and a pony is height. Any *Equus caballus* that stands shorter than 14.2 hands high is a pony. Any taller than that, and it's a horse.

But here's where things get confusing. Some breeds of horses may include smaller members who never grow more than 14.1 hands, such as Arabian and Caspian horses. Is a 14-hand Arabian a horse, or a pony? And what if a member of a pony breed grows over 14.2? It can happen. Look at the tables on these pages that give average height ranges across a sampling of horse and pony breeds. Notice anything interesting? All of the "horse" breeds have height ranges that fall below the 14.2 minimum for horses.

Telling the Difference

So, it seems that the height definition is actually a little slippery. So what, exactly, separates horses from ponies? Some people maintain that there are more differences between horses and ponies than just height. They say:

- Ponies are more surefooted than horses.
- Ponies have shorter cannon bones.
- Horses are more willing and obedient.
- Horses have finer, thinner manes and tails.

Another often-mentioned difference is: "Ponies are stockier than horses." Well, that may be true sometimes, but some breeds—like the Welsh mountain pony— aren't very stocky at all.

Pony Personality

Personality is another tricky question. Are ponies more difficult? Some people think so, adding that a pony isn't always the best choice for a child's first mount. Admittedly, a Shetland glaring at you from under its bushy forelock can be very unnerving. But maybe that's just a particularly cranky pony. Is it fair to stick the "difficult" label on all ponies?

What's in a Name?

So if you can't judge by height, and can't judge by build, and can't judge by personality, what should you use to differentiate between a horse and a pony? The name?

One problem with that idea: the polo pony is really a horse.

Connemara ponies come from Connemara, in western Ireland.

Welsh ponies might not be very big, but they're still plenty strong!

PONY BREEDS

Breed	Height
American Quarter	11.2–14.2 hh
Banker	13–14.3 hh
Connemara	13–14.2 hh
French Saddle Pony	12.1–14.2 hh
Gotland	12–14 hh
Kerry Bog	10–11 hh
Newfoundland	11–14.2 hh
Pony of the Americas	11.2–14.2 hh
Shetland	Up to 10.2 hh

Even a young Shetland pony has a thick mane.

Evolution of the Horse

Fossils are bones and other once-living material that have either turned into rock or left impressions in rocks. Fossilized individuals of a particular animal type, such as a horse, show how the animal changed over time, or evolved. This series of fossils is called the fossil record. Scientists have found an amazing array of fossils that show how the horse began, changed, and became the animal we know today. And it all started in North America, with a little tiny critter called *Hyracotherium*.

From the Dawn to the Mountain

Hyracotherium once had another scientific name: *Eohippus*, which means "dawn horse."

A hyrax rests on a sunny rock.

But this cooler name had to be dropped in favor of the difficult-to-say *Hyracotherium* (which means "hyrax-like beast." A hyrax looks like a big guinea pig but is related to the elephant—told you the name isn't as cool as *Eohippus*!). This first horse grew to about the size of a small dog. It lived during the Eocene epoch, about 55 million years ago. Unlike today's horses, which have only one toe, it had four toes on each foot, and the bones of its forearms were not fused into one.

About 2 million years after *Hyracotherium*, *Orohippus* ("mountain horse") appeared on the scene. Its forearm bones were still unfused, but its hind feet had only three toes, and the middle toe on each of its forefeet was bigger than its older relative's.

Next came *Mesohippus*, which lived about 35 million years ago, during the Oligocene epoch. This "middle horse" ran on only three toes on each foot and was starting to look more the horses that we know today, which are called *Equus*.

No More Leaves

Merychippus ("ruminant horse") looked even more like modern horses, even though it still had three toes. It lived about 15 million years ago. It had a long face, like modern horses, and long legs that let it run fast and far. Unlike its predecessors, *Merychippus* grazed

GREENLAND

NORTH AMERICA

EUROPE

ASIA

AFRICA

INDIA

SOUTH AMERICA

AUSTRALIA

ANTARCTICA

Earth During the Pliocene Epoch

The world of the Pliocene epoch looked pretty similar to today's, but it wasn't until the end of the period that North and South America joined and Africa slammed into Europe and Asia.

The tiny *Hyracotherium* is the most ancient of all horses.

on grass instead of browsing on leaves like a deer.

Horse Trumpeter?

During the Pliocene epoch, between 12 and 6 million years ago, *Pliohippus* ("horse of the Pliocene") appeared in North America. This horse is the ancestor of *Equus* and the ancestor of two other branches on the horse family tree that lived in South America (these horses died out). *Pliohippus* skulls show an interesting feature: depressions in front of the eye sockets. What were these holes for? Scientists think they may have been for lip muscles or scent glands. One scientist even proposed that they attached to *Pliohippus*'s sinuses somehow, allowing it to trumpet loudly.

Powerhouse Horse

Pliohippus's facial depressions also appear on the skull of the next fossil horse, *Dinohippus*. No, its name doesn't mean it lived at the time of the dinosaurs (they were long gone by the time horses showed up). Rather, *dino* means "powerful," so this was the "powerful horse." Some of these animals had one toe, like *Equus*, and some had three.

WEIRD BUT TRUE!

Horses can't vomit. Why? The muscular valve between a horse's esophagus and stomach, the cardiac sphincter, is so strong that it won't open unless food is passing into the stomach. In fact, the stomach will burst before the valve will give way.

THE EVOLUTION OF THE HORSE

Millions of Years Ago

Genus

Forefeet

1–present day

Equus (modern horse)

12–6

Pliohippus

15

Merychippus

35

Mesohippus

55

Hyracotherium

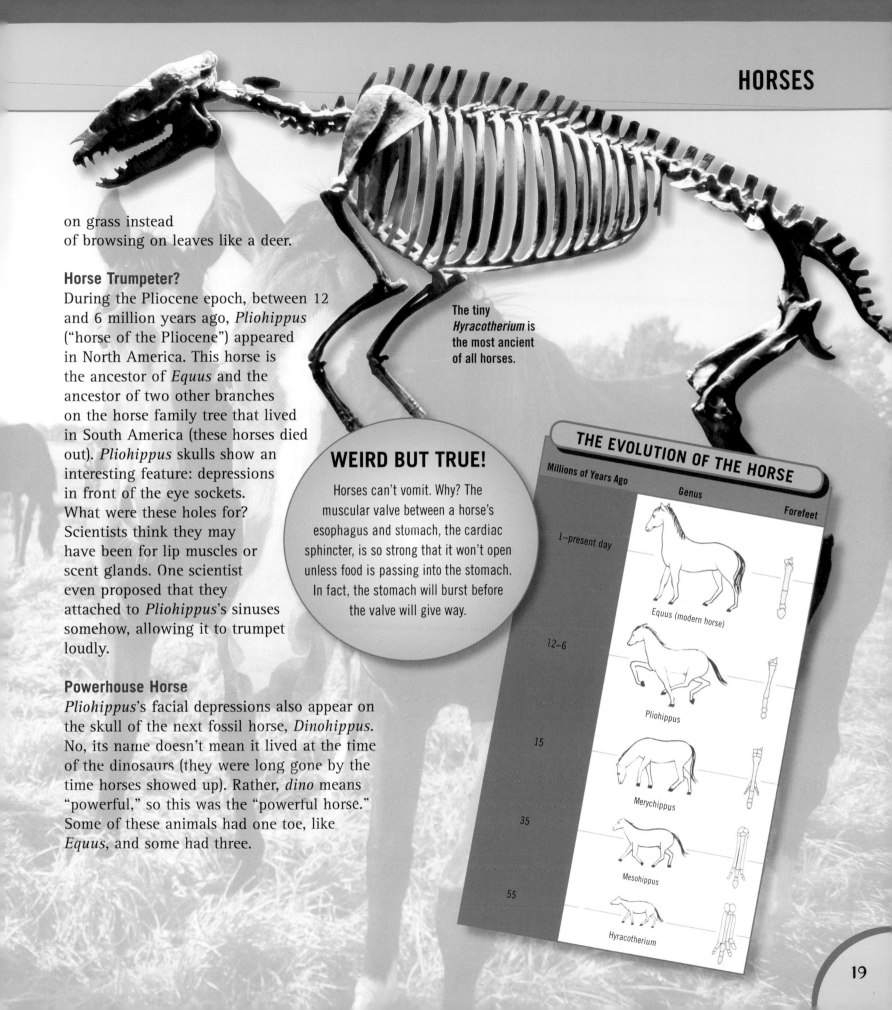

Early People and the Horse

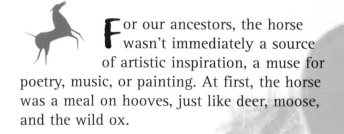

For our ancestors, the horse wasn't immediately a source of artistic inspiration, a muse for poetry, music, or painting. At first, the horse was a meal on hooves, just like deer, moose, and the wild ox.

Riding Horses

Somewhere, many years ago, an orphan foal might have become a pet. Then someone realized that that pet could be more than just good company: it was very strong, social, and could carry lots of stuff! During the Pleistocene epoch (which ended about 11 thousand years ago), this discovery was probably made and forgotten time and time again. Finally, though, the idea of riding horses, rather than just eating them, caught on. Researchers figure that this breakthrough occurred in more than one place.

Riding on horseback changed everything. The rider could move much more quickly than he ever could on foot. He could see farther because he was higher off the ground. And he could look down on anyone who wasn't mounted. Together, speed, sight, and superiority allowed horse-mounted humans to dominate groups that didn't have horses. Mounted raiders could strike fast, steal what they wanted, and vanish as quickly as they had come. There wasn't a thing their victims could do . . . except get their own horses. Stealing horses probably became a pretty popular activity, and horses became humankind's partner.

A New Best Friend

And what a versatile partner the horse became! Not only did horses allow for faster travel and those lightning-strike raids on the neighbors, but, using a harness, they could be hitched to a plow to till the soil or to a wagon to carry goods and belongings.

Why could the horse be domesticated (adapted to life with humans), while its relative the zebra couldn't? One answer involves the horse's temperament. Although some horses can be intractable (untrainable), overall, horses are willing to do what people ask—key to successful domestication.

DID YOU KNOW?

Xenophon was a Greek general and a master horseman who literally wrote the book on horse training. In it, he talked about choosing a horse, caring for it, even how to ride a spirited horse or a "dull" one. Xenophon's book is still used today—almost 2,500 years after he wrote it!

People have ridden horses to war for thousands of years.

THE HORSE IN ART

ARTISTS HAVE depicted horses for thousands of years. In prehistoric caves in France, particularly one called Lascaux, horses figure prominently among the animals pictured on the walls. The ancient humans who made these cave paintings hunted the horse for food. Their paintings show stubby brown horses with stiff black manes and white bellies.

As the relationship between horses and people changed, so did the way that artists portrayed them. The ancient Egyptians carved the horse in stone. The Egyptian horses are shown as long-legged, noble creatures pulling chariots. Horses reflect the glory of the pharaohs, who were believed to be gods. No god would be caught dead riding a stubby little creature such as those in the Lascaux paintings!

The Greeks painted images of horses in battle on pottery and carved them into the walls of the Parthenon, ancient Greek's most important temple. The Romans copied Greek art, including depicting horses in paintings and sculptures. The Chinese created statues of warhorses, complete with saddles and bridles, and buried them in tombs.

During the Middle Ages, horses appeared in beautifully illustrated books, called illuminated manuscripts, and woven tapestries. When the Middle Ages ended, artists like Michelangelo and Leonardo da Vinci revitalized realism in art and the portraits of man's partner, the horse.

Caves of the Paleolithic Age

🪦 caves

ATLANTIC OCEAN

FRANCE

Lascaux

SPAIN

Pyrenees Mountains

Southern France and northern Spain are peppered with decorated caves from the Upper Paleolithic age (40,000 to 11,000 years ago). Lascaux, with its frolicking herds of horses, is a fine example.

A marble horse head from the Parthenon. In ancient Greece, horses were noble creatures, sacred to the god Poseidon.

The mythical unicorn graces a medieval European manuscript. These fanciful horned horses still ignite our imagination.

Horses Spread Around the World

Horses evolved in North America, but they didn't stay there. At various points in world history, groups of horses migrated to Asia. But how did they get there from North America? At the time of the migrations, a land bridge connected North America and Asia. The world was in an ice age, and much of the ocean's water was frozen in glaciers. About 21,000 years ago, during the last ice age, the sea level was 400 feet

Horse and Human Migration in North America
- - - - Horse migration
———— Human migration

PACIFIC OCEAN

NORTH AMERICA

ATLANTIC OCEAN

below where it is today. (If today's oceans were 400 feet lower, you could walk from San Francisco to Oakland, and Long Island wouldn't be an island.) Alaska and Russia were joined by a broad, grassy plain—just the thing for hungry horses!

So some Ice Age horses walked out onto the plain. They grazed their way north and west, over the land bridge toward Asia. There, they found themselves in a new land full of possibilities—and since no other horses lived there, they didn't have to compete for food.

Other creatures crossed back and forth across the bridge, too, including woolly mammoths, antelopes, and humans. As the horses went north and west, people went east and south. They traveled into North America and, eventually, Central and South America, also. Curiously, not long after the humans arrived in North America, the horses died out. Scientists think that a combination of hunting (by the newly arrived humans) and climate change caused the extinction. We know the climate changed because the oceans rose and covered the land bridge. Horses wouldn't return to North America until they arrived with the Spanish in the 1500s.

Yet, the horses that had crossed the bridge kept traveling. Their descendants adapted to the different environments they encountered, some becoming small and fast, others large and sturdy. After thousands of years, people tamed horses, and the course of history changed forever.

HORSE MAKE-OVERS

EARLY HORSES were short, stocky critters, with manes that stuck up like a Mohawk haircut. They were probably brown with white bellies. In other words, they were clearly horses but could use some improvement!

That's where people come into the picture. Humans develop new breeds of animals (and change the looks of others) with selective breeding. Let's say you have a mare that has a great temperament, but her legs are really short. If you mate her to your neighbor's long-legged stallion, the foal might end up with both his mom's nice personality and his dad's long legs.

Selective breeding takes generations to create lasting changes in an animal. But it has allowed humans to develop horses that are fast, strong, amenable, and just plain gorgeous.

Horse Migration in Asia

– – – Horse migration

EUROPE

ASIA

AFRICA

PACIFIC OCEAN

An artist's depiction of a herd of Ice Age horses and woolly mammoths in Siberia.

LOOK A DEAD HORSE IN THE MOUTH

The horse has one of the most complete fossil records of all animals. That is, scientists have been able to reconstruct nearly the whole story of the horse's evolution by looking at their fossils.

One thing scientists look at is teeth. By studying the shape of a fossil horse's teeth, scientists can figure out whether it ate leaves or grass. Recent studies have done away with the idea that horses ate leaves first and then became grass-eaters. Instead, it seems that horses went back and forth several times: some older species ate grass, and more recent ones ate leaves. Seems you can learn a lot by looking a dead horse in the mouth!

The World of Horses

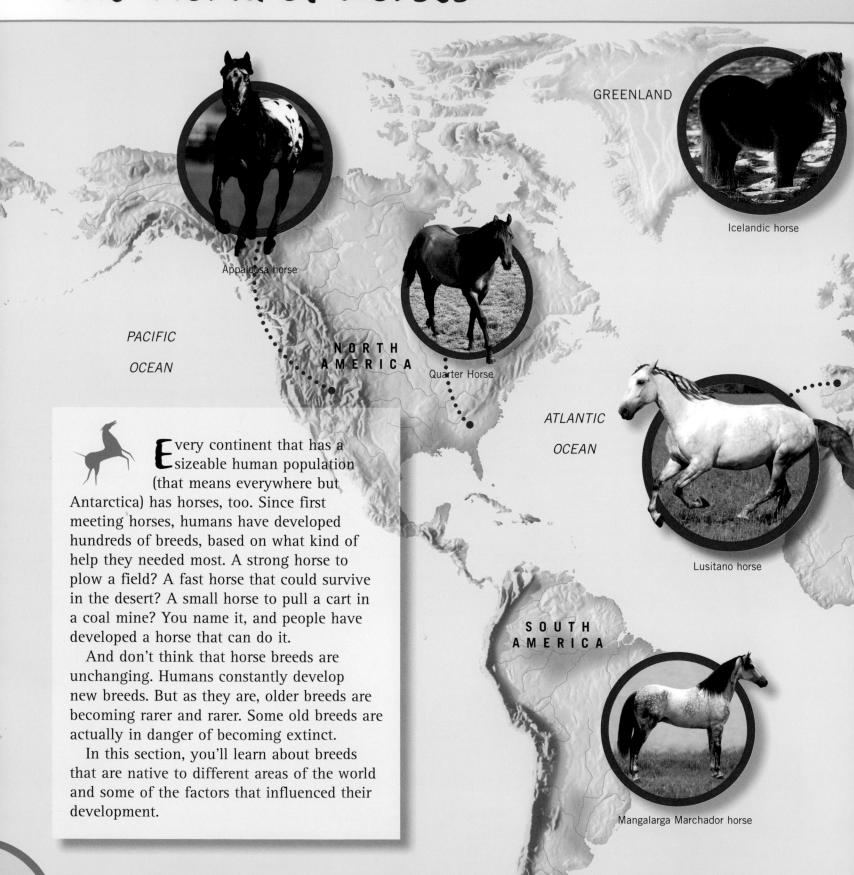

GREENLAND

Icelandic horse

PACIFIC

OCEAN

NORTH
AMERICA

Appaloosa horse

Quarter Horse

ATLANTIC

OCEAN

Lusitano horse

SOUTH
AMERICA

Mangalarga Marchador horse

Every continent that has a sizeable human population (that means everywhere but Antarctica) has horses, too. Since first meeting horses, humans have developed hundreds of breeds, based on what kind of help they needed most. A strong horse to plow a field? A fast horse that could survive in the desert? A small horse to pull a cart in a coal mine? You name it, and people have developed a horse that can do it.

And don't think that horse breeds are unchanging. Humans constantly develop new breeds. But as they are, older breeds are becoming rarer and rarer. Some old breeds are actually in danger of becoming extinct.

In this section, you'll learn about breeds that are native to different areas of the world and some of the factors that influenced their development.

Fjord horse

ARCTIC OCEAN

Budyonny horses

Lipizzaner horse

E U R O P E

Akhal-Teke horse

A S I A

Marwari horse

A F R I C A

Arabian horse

INDIAN

OCEAN

A U S T R A L I A

Brumby horse

Nooitgedacht pony

Hot Blood of the Desert

An Islamic legend says that one day, Allah (the god of Islam) gathered a handful of the wind. He blew on the wind, and it condensed to form the horse. Although it is just a legend, this story reflects the beauty and spirit of one of the world's most famous and impressive horses: the Arabian breed.

The Origins of the "Oriental Horse"

The West Asian environment is challenging for many living things. Without human care, it is an unlikely place for a horse to survive. But the people of ancient Persia (modern Iraq, Iran, Turkey, and Syria) bred a horse that would not only survive but thrive in the hot climate. These horses were first called "Oriental" horses, but today we know them as Turks, Barbs (though Barbs were actually from Morocco in Africa, not Western Asia), and Arabians.

The Bedouin, a group of nomadic desert dwellers, are partly responsible for the Arabian horse. The Bedouins bred their horses carefully. The prominent forehead, or Jibbah, was a mark of the blessings of Allah (the more bulgy the forehead, the more blessings it was believed to hold). The flaglike tail showed pride and the arched neck, courage. A Bedouin could recite the lineage of his horses as easily as he could his own ancestry.

Worldwide Popularity

These hot-blooded desert horses changed history. They allowed not only the Bedouins to seize property from other tribes, but also helped Egyptian pharaohs to extend their empires, influenced the rise of the Roman Empire, and enabled Eastern invaders to take over parts of Europe. The Europeans had no horses fast enough to compete with the hot-bloods. But as soon as possible, they got their hands on those horses! Today, almost every horse breed has been improved by the

An Arabian stallion with a large Jibbah. He has the large eyes and fine head shape characteristic of the breed.

MORE BREEDS OF WESTERN ASIA

Breed	Origin
Araba	Turkey
Canik	Turkey
Cirit	Turkey
Cukurova	Turkey
Giawf	Yemen
Hinis	Turkey
Nagdi	Yemen
Persian Arab	Iran
Plateau Persian	Iran
Syrian Arab	Syria
Trakya	Turkey
Uzunyayla	Turkey
Yamud	Iran
Yemen	Yemen

addition of Arabian blood at some time in its history. Although some people say that the Arabian is a unique subspecies, it is actually a breed—a very old breed, but a breed nevertheless.

A Bedouin man with a prize Nejd horse

TURKEY

Caspian Sea

SYRIA

IRAQ

IRAN

Zagros Mountains

JORDAN

EGYPT

Red Sea

The Plateau of Nejd

U.A.E.

SAUDI ARABIA

OMAN

YEMEN

ETHIOPIA

The Israeli horse breed must contend with harsh climates.

The shores of the Caspian Sea are home to the Caspian horse.

THE MANE FACTS: ARABIAN

Height: 14–15.3 hh

Physical appearance: Very beautiful, with a dished profile and large eyes. Long, arched neck. high-set tail.

Qualities: Tremendous endurance and speed

Uses: Showing, pleasure riding, endurance competition

Colors: Bay, black, chestnut, gray, or roan. White markings are permitted.

Cool stuff: Arabians have black skin, even if their hair isn't black.

African Steeds, Tough Breeds

Africa is a tough place to be a horse. First, several species of large, hungry predators, like lions, leopards, and hyenas, are happy to make a meal of you. Then there's the heat and the world's largest hot desert, the Sahara. If that's not enough, a killer disease spread by mosquitoes adds to the trouble. Despite all these unpleasant aspects, horses have become a part of the African landscape.

Horses weren't known in most of Africa until the arrival of Europeans in the fifteenth century. But the people who lived in North Africa—like the ancient Egyptians—knew about horses and used them often. (Archaeologists

have found evidence that horses have been in this area for thousands of years.) The Barb, a breed developed in Morocco, Algeria, and Tunisia, is a tough, fast horse that can survive in harsh conditions. In 711, the North African Moors invaded Spain and easily defeated the Spanish because they were mounted on swift Barbs. The surefooted Barbs could charge headlong down steep slopes that other horses shied away from. The Moors weren't the last army to ride these remarkable horses. Napoleon Bonaparte's forces rode Barbs in the early

A finely config-
ured Barb horse
with origins in
northern Africa

MORE BREEDS OF AFRICA

Breed	Origin
Abyssinian	Ethiopia
Barh-el-Ghazal	Chad
Basuto	Lesotho
Bobo	Ivory Coast
Boer	South Africa
Hausa	Niger
Mbai	Chad
M'Par	Senegal
Nefza	Tunisia
Pony Mousseye	Cameroon

The Berber people from northern
Africa favor Barb horses.

1800s, and during World War II the only members of the German army that managed to reach Moscow, Russia, weren't in tanks or trucks—they were riding Barbs!

The Barb has had more influence on other breeds than any breed except the Arabian. It was used to develop the Andalusian, Spanish Barb, Quarter Horse, Paso Fino, and Criollo, among others. Unfortunately, there's been so much crossbreeding with Arabians that finding a purebred Barb is hard to do.

ATLANTIC
OCEAN

A F R I C A

NAMIBIA

SOUTH AFRICA

Namib Desert horse,
Namibia

Nooitgedacht pony,
South Africa

SOUTH AFRICA MAKES A HORSE

Question: *What is a camel?*
Answer: *A horse planned by a committee.*

This joke suggests that working in groups doesn't always pan out well, but there really is a breed of horse that was planned by a committee. It's the Nooitgedacht ("Nue-it-ged-awk-t") of South Africa.

South African authorities set up a horse-planning committee in 1951. The committee had two goals: develop an indigenous or native horse breed, and preserve the Basuto, a hardy breed that had nearly been wiped out because its popularity had resulted in massive exportation of the breed, until few members were left at home.

The committee selected the horses that would be used to start the new breed, including its foundation stallion, named Vonk. In addition to Basutos, Boer and Arabian horses made it into the mix. Over nearly 20 years, researchers worked to develop the new horse, incorporating only a quarter of the horses that the breeding program produced. In 1968, their new breed, the Nooitgedacht, was ready for a breed association.

The Nooitgedacht is a pony suitable for riding and light draft work. It has the Basuto's bravery and is a loving and loyal mount for children and adults alike.

Best of all, despite its committee-based origins, the Nooitgedacht doesn't look anything like a camel.

29

Early War, Early Horses

The horse changed the way that human beings traveled. Stronger and faster than dogs or people, horses could carry large loads over long distances. They opened up trade and communication among groups that had previously had little contact.

Unfortunately, horses also made it easier to wage war.

A 4,500-year-old picture shows chariots pulled by donkeys in ancient Mesopotamia. Horses would soon replace donkeys.

A man on a horse has a huge advantage. He is faster than his enemy. When his horse gallops forward, it increases the strength behind his spear throw. And the horse itself is a barrier, preventing an enemy on foot from reaching its rider.

Warriors on Wheels

Soon after domestication, people quickly learned that a horse was a tremendous military weapon. At first, warriors hitched horses to chariots (horseback riding hadn't yet been developed). The first chariots rolled on four wheels and were hard to steer, but by 1600 BCE, the two-wheeled chariot had been invented. Carrying a soldier and a driver, two-wheeled chariots proved fast and maneuverable. Chariots were used by such diverse cultures as the ancient Egyptians, Hittites, Chinese, and Celts. In ancient Rome, horses carried fresh soldiers into battle and weary warriors out of the fray, while chariot racing became a major spectator sport.

Horses in War

The chariot faded from the battlefield when mounted cavalry became the norm. Strong, well-trained horses carried fighters swiftly into battle. It took brave and well-trained foot soldiers to stand their ground against the onslaught of mounted cavalry.

The extreme of cavalry was probably the armored knight of the Middle Ages in Europe, but horses continued to go to war as late as the twentieth century. Beginning in World War II, trucks, tanks, and Humvees began to replace horses in modern warfare. Yet these armored divisions are still called "cavalry."

It doesn't look much like a horse, but this World War II tank was called cavalry.

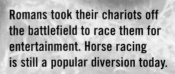

Romans took their chariots off the battlefield to race them for entertainment. Horse racing is still a popular diversion today.

30

A statue of Alexander the Great pays tribute to both the conqueror and his steed.

THE MIGHTY MOUNTED MACEDONIANS!

PHILIP II OF MACEDON and his son, Alexander, broke the rules. While everybody else was tooling around in chariots, they were leading mounted cavalry forces on their way to conquering half of their world.

Philip II united Macedonia, an area that included parts of Greece, Bulgaria, and the Republic of Macedonia. From there, his son took over. Alexander the Great conquered Egypt, Syria, northwestern India, Pakistan, and part of Afghanistan (then called Bactria). Renowned for his horsemanship, Alexander owned a horse, Bucephalus, who became nearly as famous as his owner. Alexander had grown up with Bucephalus and rode him in every battle until the brave horse died after a battle in 326 BCE. In remembrance, Alexander named a city after the horse (modern-day Jhelum, in Pakistan).

The Empire of Alexander, 323 BCE

Alexander's Empire

EUROPE

Black Sea

Macedonia

Caspian Sea

ASIA

Mediterranean Sea

Syria

Bactria

Bacephala (Jhelum)

EGYPT

Arabian Peninsula

Red Sea

INDIA

AFRICA

Arabian Sea

The Empire of Atilla the Hun, 5th Century CE

Atilla's Empire

ASIA

EUROPE

AFRICA

THE MASTER HORSEMEN

No discussion of mounted warriors is complete without a mention of the Huns. Hailing from beyond the Volga River, the Huns swept across Asia and much of Europe during the fourth and fifth centuries.

And how did they do it? They were master horsemen. It's said that the Huns invented the stirrup, which allowed them to stand up and fire their arrows at the enemy (it also made falling off a lot less likely). Fearless and ferocious warriors, they defeated the Visigoths, the people of the Balkans, and the Romans. Finally, the Huns and their infamous leader, Attila, were beaten in France—nearly 1,800 miles west from where they started. After Attila died, the Hunnic empire fell apart. Yet, they and their skills with horses have never been forgotten.

Stirrups are used around the world, nearly 1,500 years after the Huns invented them.

The Changing Horses of Europe

The horse didn't become really valuable in Europe until two important inventions arrived from elsewhere: the stirrup and the horse collar.

The Stirrup Builds Europe

The stirrup was invented by the Huns, a nomadic people famed for their horsemanship. By simply giving the rider somewhere to put his feet, the stirrup gave the rider extra support and allowed him to sit more securely in the saddle. Because they were less likely to fall off, people began to ride more often. Without the stirrup, the armored knight of the Middle Ages would never have existed—and by extension, neither would the feudal system of knights, peasants, and kings that led to modern Europe!

From Horse to Market

The horse collar came from China, arriving in Europe about 600 years after the Chinese invented it sometime around the second century CE. It replaced older, less effective harnesses and the yokes of oxen. With this device, horses could pull plows and wagons about half again as fast as oxen could. As a result, farmers could grow more food than they needed for their own families. They were able to sell the extra produce, leading to the growth of markets and a merchant class—an important step to the modern age.

Warming the Blood

Early European horses were strong and sturdy, suited for pulling wagons and carrying knights. Only after the

MORE BREEDS OF EUROPE

Breed	Origin
Alter Real	Portugal
Ardennais	France
Dutch Warmblood	Netherlands
Finnhorse	Finland
Gotland	Sweden
Jutland	Denmark
Knabstrup	Denmark
Konih	Poland
Noriker	Austria
Oldenburg	Germany
Salerno	Italy
Selle Français	France
Skyros	Greece
Swedish Warmblood	Sweden

A Percheron horse in a modern collar

Moors invaded Spain on swift little Barbs did the Europeans consider changing their horses. By crossing their cold-blooded heavy horses with the hot-blooded breeds, they produced breeds that were stronger than the Barbs, swifter than the heavy horses, and suited for a variety of purposes.

Today, European warm-blooded horses excel in international competition, especially jumping and dressage events.

HORSES IN WORLD WAR I

At the start of World War I, Germany and Great Britain each mounted about 100,000 cavalry. But this war—unlike all the wars in the past—didn't feature open fields to charge across. The deep trenches of World War I made cavalry charges useless. Worse, the new machine gun could cut down even the bravest horses. At the end of one battle in 1918, only 4 horses survived out of 150 that had charged a machine-gun nest.

During the war, horses were used mostly for transport. They pulled wagons, ambulances, and cannons through battles, mud, and air filled with poison gas. About 8 million horses died during this "war to end all wars." As one soldier said of the horses, "We knew what we were there for. Them poor devils didn't, did they?"

Belgian draft horse, Belgium

Friesian horse, Netherlands

ATLANTIC OCEAN

E U R O P E

Konik horse and foal, Poland

Horses pull wagons alongside German troops in World War I.

Mediterranean Sea

A F R I C A

Haflinger horse, Austria

Hanoverian horse, Germany

Andalusian horse, Spain

The Leaping Lipizzan

The majestic horses file into the arena, the only sound the soft *pft* of their hooves. The crowd is silent. The performance, a combination of battle maneuvers and elegant movements, is about to begin!

Welcome to the Spanish Riding School in Vienna, Austria, home to the Lipizzaner stallions. For more than 400 years, the school has showcased the finest equestrian performances in the world. All the horses that perform are stallions. Stallions can be aggressive and very hard to handle. These Lipizzaner stallions, however, are true "gentlemen."

Just because they're gentlemen doesn't mean they're wimps. Their ancestors were war horses. On the battlefield, they used special movements to protect their riders and to scare the daylights out of enemy soldiers. These movements are known today as "airs above the ground."

All Lipizzaners are born at a farm in Piber, Austria. Most are born black, with the occasional bay. As they get older, they turn gray and white. Each is considered a national treasure, and until recently, Lipizzaners were government property. The riding school is now independent, but Lipizzaners are still a source of great pride in Austria.

AIRS ABOVE THE GROUND

IN THE LEVADE movement, the horse stands still, on its hind legs, at a 45-degree angle. The levade requires tremendous strength (remember, the horse weighs half a ton!), control, and balance. In battle, the rider could slash at enemy foot soldiers with his sword as his mount held the levade.

In the capriole movement, the horse leaps straight up into the air and kicks out with his hind legs. That sure would have made any enemy soldiers back off quickly!

The most difficult and spectacular air above the ground is the courbette. In it, the horse stands on his hind legs and leaps forward, landing on his hind legs again and again. The courbette allowed the horse and rider to break through an infantry line. Only the strongest horses manage this move!

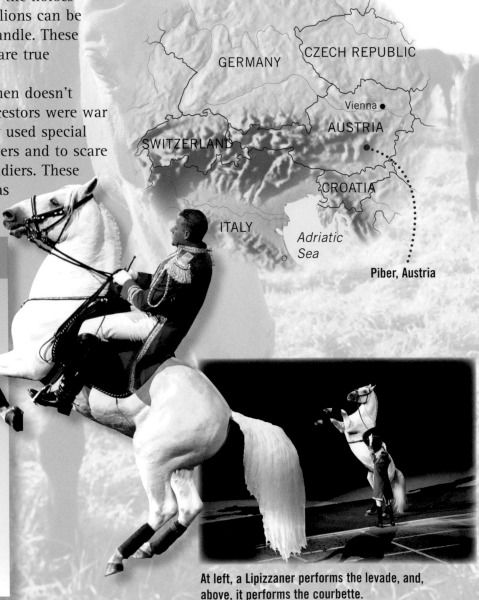

GERMANY
CZECH REPUBLIC
Vienna
AUSTRIA
SWITZERLAND
CROATIA
ITALY
Adriatic
Sea
Piber, Austria

At left, a Lipizzaner performs the levade, and, above, it performs the courbette.

DID YOU KNOW?

Not everyone can be a rider at the Spanish Riding School. Riders must apply and hope for acceptance. And even that's just the beginning. Riders must train for up to 14 years, with the oldest horses teaching the newest riders.

THE MANE FACTS: LIPIZZAN

Height: 15–16.1 hh
Physical appearance: Head is long with a convex or straight profile; muscular, arched neck; withers are rather flat and the back is long; chest is deep and wide, with powerful shoulders and quarters; legs are strong.
Qualities: Intelligent, eager to please
Uses: Riding, especially dressage
Colors: Adults are almost always white, sometimes gray, although born black. Rarely foals are born bay, and they do not change color.
Cool stuff: All Lipizzans for the riding school are born at Piber. For years, only men could ride in Spanish Riding School performances, but now women can, too!

THE RESCUE OF THE LIPIZZANS

During World War II, Germany conquered Austria. Although the Germans allowed the Spanish Riding School to operate, it was no longer part of a free Vienna. In 1945, allied forces began bombing Vienna. The leader of the Spanish Riding School, Colonel Alois Podjahsky, evacuated his precious horses to a private estate 200 miles from the city. Even there, the horses were not safe. The Russian Army—which had a reputation for destruction—was closing in fast. Podjahsky knew the Lipizzans were in terrible danger.

Fortunately, General George Patton—leader of the American forces—was an old friend of Colonel Podjahsky's. When Patton found out about the dire situation facing the Lipizzans, he had the horses declared wards of the United States Army. Without Patton's quick actions, chances are good that the Lipizzan breed would have been yet another victim of the war.

THE SIX SIRES

Every Lipizzaner can trace its ancestry back to one or more of the foundation sires:
- Pluto, a gray Danish horse foaled in 1765
- Conversano, a black Neopolitan horse foaled in 1767
- Favory, a dun Lipizzan foaled in 1779
- Neapolitano, a brown Neapolitan foaled in 1790
- Siglavy, a gray Arabian foaled in 1810
- Maestoso, a gray half-Lipizzan, half-Spanish horse foaled in 1819

This Lipizzaner and his rider are ready for the show.

Islands of Horses

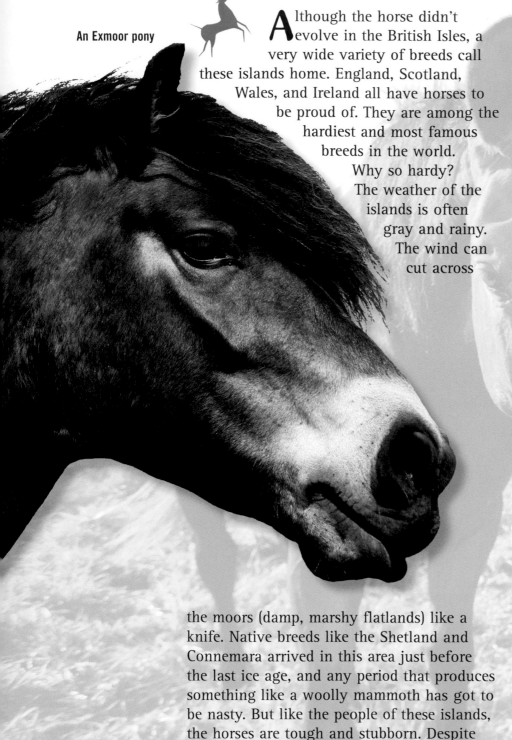

An Exmoor pony

Although the horse didn't evolve in the British Isles, a very wide variety of breeds call these islands home. England, Scotland, Wales, and Ireland all have horses to be proud of. They are among the hardiest and most famous breeds in the world. Why so hardy? The weather of the islands is often gray and rainy. The wind can cut across the moors (damp, marshy flatlands) like a knife. Native breeds like the Shetland and Connemara arrived in this area just before the last ice age, and any period that produces something like a woolly mammoth has got to be nasty. But like the people of these islands, the horses are tough and stubborn. Despite the climate, they have eked out an existence—and even thrived.

Horse Sports

The people of the British Isles are known for a love of horses and horse sports. Foxhunting, also called "riding to the hounds," developed in England. The object of foxhunting is not so much to kill the fox (though that does happen) but to test rider and horse on a challenging cross-country course. The typical course involves fences, rivers, ditches, thorny bushes, and rocks. It's still popular, even in the United States. Besides foxhunting, the gymkhana (pronounced jim-KA-na), games on horseback, is very popular, as is racing. Fine carriage horse breeds, such as the Hackney, were developed in the British Isles, too.

From sturdy Shetlands to clean-legged Suffolks and heavily feathered Shires, the horses of Britain are a widely diverse bunch!

THE MANE FACTS: EXMOOR PONY

Height: 11.2 to 12.3 hh

Physical appearance: A stocky, strong animal, the Exmoor pony exhibits two unique traits: a mealy muzzle and a toad eye. *Ew*, you might be thinking. But don't worry—there's nothing wrong with either. A "mealy" muzzle is just grayish. The "toad eye" is a colorful description for a fleshy upper eyelid that is supposed to act like the visor on a baseball cap and keep rain out of the pony's eyes. If that's not enough, it also has a "snow chute," which is just a name for a fan of short hairs near the root of the tail.

Qualities: Hardy and tough, these ponies have been known to carry loads of nearly 170 pounds. Their waterproof winter coats helps them survive the harsh climate of the moors.

Uses: Pack animals, riding, driving

Color: Brown. In fact, they all look almost identical.

Cool stuff: This pony is thought to be the oldest pure descendant of ponies that lived in the British Isles 100,000 years ago!

MORE BREEDS OF THE BRITISH ISLES

Breed	Origin
Cleveland Bay	England
Dales pony	England
Eriskay pony	Scotland
Exmoor pony	England
Fell pony	England
Hackney pony	England
Hackney	England
Irish cob	Ireland
Irish draught	Ireland
Rhum Island pony	Scotland
Suffolk	England
Welsh pony*	Wales

*The Welsh pony actually includes four sub-breeds: The Welsh mountain pony, the Welsh pony, the Welsh pony of cob type, and the Welsh cob.

Highland ponies, Scotland

Shetland pony, Shetland Islands

The British Isles

United Kingdom

Shetland Islands

Orkney Islands

Hebrides

ATLANTIC OCEAN

SCOTLAND

DID YOU KNOW?

Shire horses carried knights into battle during the Middle Ages, but ever since have enjoyed life on the farm!

Connemara ponies, Ireland

IRELAND

Isle of Man

Irish Sea

Dublin

North Sea

WALES

ENGLAND

London

Celtic Sea

Shire horse, England

Irish sport horse, Ireland

Welsh pony, Wales

New Forest pony, England

A Knight's Horse

During the Middle Ages, knights in armor dominated the battlefields of Europe. A knight, trained from the age of seven to fight on horseback, was like a human tank. Because of the heavy armor he wore for protection, he couldn't ride just any horse—and without a horse that could carry him, a knight was just a guy in a metal suit.

In the Right Hand

A knight's warhorse was called a destrier. The name comes from French words that mean "in the right hand," because a knight's servant, or squire, would lead the horse by holding its reins in his right hand. Destriers were mighty horses that could travel all day at a trot and were fearless among the chaos and noise of battle.

THE DESTRIERS

For the horse, the knight and his equipment created a burden of up to 300 pounds. That's why those horses were so big, with strong legs and calm temperaments that kept them from panicking in battle. The Great Flemish horse, the La Perch horse, and the English Great Horse all carried knights into battle. Today, their descendants are the Belgian, the Percheron, and the Shire.

Barding for Horses

Just as a knight wore armor, so did his horse—after all, sword strikes and arrows fell just as often on the horse as they did on the rider. The horse's armor was made of heavy fabric; a hard, boiled leather called *cuir bouilli*; regular leather; chain mail; or metal plate. Horse armor was called barding.

The horse also wore plate armor to protect the face and head. This armor was called a *chanfron*. The *chanfron* might hold a feathered plume, the knight's heraldic mark (a sort of pictorial name tag), or a short spike over the horse's forehead. Overlapping metal plates, called *crinets*, protected the neck, while allowing it maneuverability. A piece called the *peytral* protected the horse's chest and shoulders.

Some saddles had very high cantles, or backs, to help the knight stay mounted during jousts or battle. Later models lowered the cantle—perhaps too many knights suffered back injuries from the high cantle. Metal plates called *flanchards* sometimes covered the saddle. Pieces called the crupper and the *garde-queue* (GARD-cue) covered the rump and the base of the tail.

All this armor had to be lined with leather or cotton fabric to protect the horse's skin from being rubbed raw (his rider's armor was lined too, for the same reason). A fabric trapper covered the whole outfit to keep it from getting wet. The trapper was usually made in the same distinctive pattern as the knight's coat of arms.

Knights and their horses wore matching gear not only for fashion, but also to identify themselves. On crowded battlefields, knights needed to quickly tell friend from foe!

chanfron

crinets

HOW DO YOU LIFT A KNIGHT?

MOVIES AND BOOKS sometimes depict knights as weighing so much that they couldn't mount a horse without the help of a crane, or even get up if they fell. In reality, knights were athletic and used to wearing their armor. They could even dance in it! A helpless knight wriggling on his back like an oversized turtle? Didn't happen.

A full suit of armor weighed 60 to 70 pounds (about the weight of an 8- or 9-year-old child). The armor around the lower body was made of smaller plates, much like the horse's neckpiece, so the knight could flex his body to mount his horse.

Later, when some armor included a helmet that bolted into place, getting mounted or getting up was impossible without help. The knights couldn't bend their necks. Their problem wasn't being too heavy, it was being too stiff!

cantle

crupper

HORSE ARMOR

peytral

lining

39

Masters of Mountain and Desert

Russia was one of the first places where prehistoric horses met humans. A huge country, Russia experiences extreme temperatures. Frozen soil permanently covers some places, broiling deserts scorch others, and thick forests obscure still more! For the people who tamed the ancient horses of this diverse land, survival was the key. Speed was secondary, and beauty—well, let's just say that beauty doesn't keep you warm at night or feed you in the desert.

Russia's horses are perfectly suited to the extremes of their homeland. Russian steppe horses, such as the Don, live where the winter temperature regularly falls to 60 degrees below zero and the summer temperature rises to 120 degrees above. Harnessed to a troika, a three-horse carriage, steppe horses pulled

ARCTIC OCEAN

EUROPE

ASIA

RUSSIA

TURKEY

KAZAKHSTAN

UZBEKISTAN

IRAQ

TURKMENISTAN

IRAN

MONGOLIA

CHINA

JAPAN

NORTH KOREA

SOUTH KOREA

Climate Zones

- desert
- steppes
- cold continental (humid)
- cold continental (dry)
- tundra

High desert plateaus are unwelcoming places even in good weather, but horses adapted to these and other harsh landscapes.

THE NATURAL GAITS

All horses have four natural gaits, which are different ways that they move. "Natural" means that they do not need training to perform these moves. Even wild horses will move in the following ways.

1. **Walk.** This gait, with an average speed of 4 miles per hour, is a four-beat movement. This means that the horse's legs move up in a sequence of left hind leg, left front leg, right hind leg, and right front leg, in a 1-2-3-4 rhythm. When walking, the horse will always have one foot off the ground and the other three on it.

2. **Trot.** The trot is a two-beat gait that varies widely in speed but averages about 8 miles per hour. When trotting, a horse's legs move in diagonal pairs, which means that if the right front leg is up, the left back leg is, too, and vice versa.

3. **Canter.** The canter, which is faster than most trots, but slower than a gallop, is a three-beat gait. In this gait, one of the rear legs propels the horse forward, making the first beat. If the horse started on its right hind leg, in the second beat, the left rear and the right front will hit the ground. On the last beat, the left front leg hits the ground while the left rear and right front are still there, too.

4. **Gallop**. The fastest of the gaits, the gallop averages from 25 to 30 miles per hour. This four-beat gait is the only one in which all of the horse's hooves are off the ground at the same time.

their owners safely home, despite blinding snowstorms, rough terrain, or hungry wolves.

The mountain horses, such as the Kabardin, are used to walking knife-edge trails that would terrify other horses—if those horses could breathe in the thin air found at nearly 10,000 feet above sea level. The mountain breeds have such hard hooves that they seldom need shoes.

Asian desert horses, such as the Akhal-Teke from Turkmenistan, survive in high temperatures with little water or food. They have thrived for more than 3,000 years, making the Akhal-Teke one of the oldest breeds of horse in the world. (It also happens to be a real beauty.)

Because of the variety of landforms and climate in their homelands, the breeds of northern Asia and Eastern Europe are noted for their endurance and survival skills.

Akhal-Teke horses seem to bond to a single person, and horse people know them as "one-rider" horses.

Akhal-Teke horses are famous for nearly limitless endurance but are also popular pleasure mounts.

RUSSIA'S GAITED HORSE

The Bashkir of Russia is one of the breeds known as a gaited breed. A horse of a gaited breed can perform more gaits than just the natural four. A Bashkir can perform up to six gaits.

The extra gaits come naturally to this sturdy, small horse, which is mostly used for riding, light draft (hauling), milk, and meat. They include the rack, in which the horse puts all its weight on one foot while the other three are off the ground. In the pace, the left legs move forward at the same time, followed by the right legs. In the Cossack trot, the horse throws its legs to the side to get through tough terrain. These extra gaits were probably appreciated by the soldiers who rode Bashkirs against Napoleon's invading army in 1812. The Russians defeated Napoleon and most returned home to Moscow in one piece, thanks to their tough, smart, loyal Bashkirs.

The Cossacks were famed for their skill with horses and even rode standing on the saddle.

English Tack

DID YOU KNOW?

Although it may sound like something you don't want to sit on, tack is the name of saddles, bridles, bits, and other equipment the horse wears for riding.

Despite the name, English tack is used around the world. English saddles come in a wide variety of shapes and sizes, but they all look basically the same: they have two flaps that hang down the horse's sides and a seat placed with the pommel high over the horse's withers. The seat scoops down in the middle, where the rider sits, and curves higher again in the back (the cantle).

There are several kinds of English saddles. The forward-seat saddle is designed for jumping. Its knee rolls help the rider grip, not slip, as the horse flies over fences. Tiny versions of English saddles are used on racehorses. These little jockey saddles weigh only about one and a half pounds (not counting the stirrups, or irons).

You might think that the "show saddle" is for riding in horse shows, and you'd be

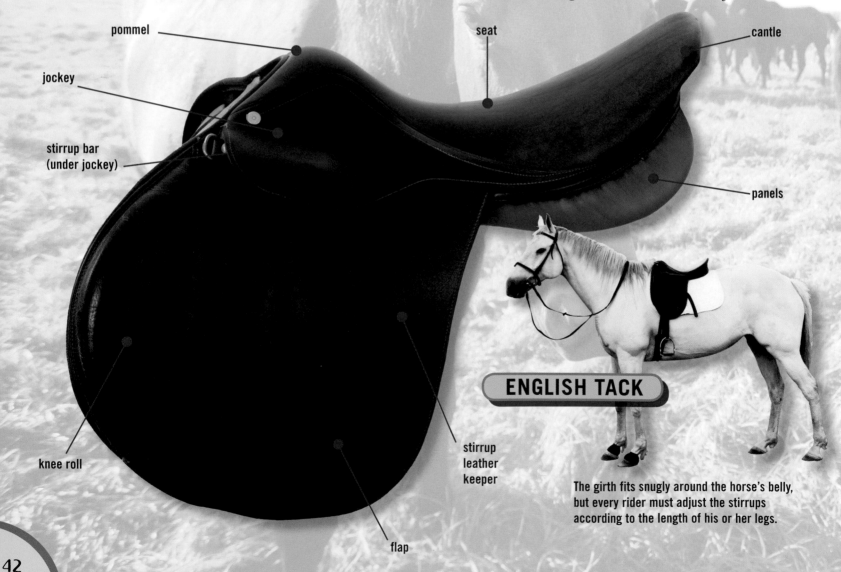

pommel

jockey

stirrup bar
(under jockey)

knee roll

flap

seat

cantle

panels

stirrup
leather
keeper

ENGLISH TACK

The girth fits snugly around the horse's belly, but every rider must adjust the stirrups according to the length of his or her legs.

partly right. This saddle is designed for riders of Saddlebred and Tennessee Walker horses. These breeds have special gaits and carry their necks high, and show saddles help position their riders correctly.

A dressage saddle is designed for horses and riders competing in dressage. In dressage, the rider controls the horse with tiny signals, pressing lightly with the legs, slightly twitching the reins, or shifting in the saddle. A well-practiced dressage team makes it seem as though the horse moves through the course all on its own, while the rider just sits still.

Whatever its size or function, all English saddles are attached to the horse with a girth, a wide strap that hugs the horse's belly. The rider attaches the girth to the billets (wide straps hidden under the flaps) with buckles. The stirrups hang from stirrup leathers that attach at the stirrup bar.

Although they're called irons, stirrups are really made out of steel. A rubber or textured metal pad holds the foot in place.

Jockeys travel light—keeping their weight down helps their horses run as fast as possible.

A BIT OF CONTROL

TO CONTROL THE HORSE, one tool the rider uses (besides legs, weight, and voice), is the bridle and bit. The bridle, or headstall, fits on the horse's head. The bit is a metal device that fits in its mouth. Together, bit and bridle help the rider use the reins to control the horse. In English riding, the reins go into the rider's hand between the pinky and third finger and out between the thumb and pointer finger. The horse feels any pressure on the reins instantly. In the hands of the wrong rider, bit and reins can cause a lot of pain!

The English saddle allows for close contact between horse and rider.

WHAT A PAIN IN THE BUTT!

Every saddle has a tree. It's the frame the saddle is built on. It can be wood, steel, fiberglass, or aluminum. The earliest saddles weren't much more than a bare wooden tree, which led to a lot of sore butts. Today, both rider and horse are protected from potential pain by layers of foam rubber and leather. Ah, that's better!

Asian Diversity

The world's largest continent after Antarctica, Asia's topography varies widely. It is home to islands and swamps, forests and tundra, deserts and windswept mountains. Accordingly, a wide variety of horse breeds have developed over the years, each suited to the needs of the people who bred it.

On the Roof of the World

Tibet is a high, mountainous place, where the air is so thin that many horses cannot survive. But the Tibetan pony is perfectly suited to its mountain home. Like the people of Tibet, it is acclimated to, or is used to, an altitude that leaves others gasping. Tibetan ponies have been known to carry loads of

Mongolian horse, Mongolia

Misaki horses, Japan

Yunnan horse, China

Tibetan pony, China

Marwari horse, India

RUSSIA

KAZAKHSTAN

MONGOLIA

JAPAN

NORTH KOREA
SOUTH KOREA

ASIA

PAKISTAN

CHINA

PACIFIC OCEAN

INDIA

BURMA

THAILAND

more than 100 pounds for 20 miles from 10,000 feet to 16,000 feet without stopping to rest, a feat unequalled in the horse world!

The Horses of War

Think of India and you may think of elephants, but the peoples of India have been riding horses for nearly 5,000 years. One group, the Rathores, developed the Marwari, a warhorse of incredible bravery and beauty. It was said that a Marwari would never return from the battlefield in defeat. It would return victorious or carrying its wounded rider, or it would not return at all. The Marwari is easy to identify: its ears curve inward to nearly meet at the tips.

In the Emperor's Garden

The people of China also rode horses into war, but a small breed held a special place in the heart of the emperor. This was the Guoxia, a naturally tiny horse (only 9 to 10 hands). Originally, the Guoxia helped with the fruit harvest by standing under the trees. People climbed the trees, picked the fruit, and dropped it into baskets on the horses' backs. Its name even means "under fruit tree horse." It eventually moved out of the orchards and into the imperial court, where it was a pet. This breed is very old, and sculptures of it have been found that are more than 2,000 years old.

This bronze statue depicts a horse wearing a saddle and dates to the Han dynasty (206 BCE to 220 CE).

MORE BREEDS OF ASIA

Breed	Origin
Buohai	China
Cheju	Korea
Chummarti	Tibet
Griffin	Mongolia
Guizhou	China
Herati	Afghanistan
Hokkaido	Japan
Noma	Japan
Sandan	China
Spiti	India
Tanghan	Nepal
Tattu	Nepal
Unmol	India
Yabu	Afghanistan

Terracotta horses from the tomb of the first emperor of China

CHINESE HORSES

Sometimes tombs hold a lot more than skeletons. The tomb of the first Chinese emperor contained 6,000 terracotta (clay) warriors and horses, as well as two bronze chariots, complete with life-size horses. Wearing detailed tack and harnesses, the horse sculptures prove that the Chinese were using tack as long ago as 221 BCE.

Riding Down Under

Without human help, horses never would have reached the island countries of the South Pacific, such as Indonesia, Australia, and New Zealand. There are no land bridges to walk over, and the ocean distances are too long to swim. So, horses, and their people, took boats.

Today, 12 horse breeds hail from Indonesia, 4 from Australia, and 1 from the Philippines. New Zealand is home to the Kaimanawa wild horse, a blend of Welsh, Exmoor, and Comet ponies, and larger breeds. About 500 Kaimanawa horses exist today.

Australia's most famous breed is the Waler horse. Developed in New South Wales (hence the name), these horses earned their fame during World War I, when they were used as cavalry mounts. They were brave and had tremendous endurance, even on short rations of food and water. One Waler, known as Bill, carried five Australian soldiers to safety after Turkish forces overran their outpost. The horse galloped for a mile over soft sand as three men rode on his back, and two others stood in the stirrups. For his bravery, Bill served out his term of duty as an officer's pack horse (carrying gear and supplies).

The success of the Waler nearly led to its extinction. Australia exported more than 100,000 Walers for war use. Quarantine laws, which restrict the movement of living things across international borders, prevented the horses that survived from returning home. Their numbers depleted, Walers started to disappear.

So does the Waler still exist? Some say the breed is extinct, but others maintain that a mere 1,000 of these gallant horses remain, either running wild or in the hands of private breeders. Because it derived from a variety of breeds that have changed over the years, the original Waler type would be impossible to re-create. The Waler lives on, however, in the blood of the Australian stock horse, a versatile breed that includes Thoroughbred and Quarter Horse blood as well.

Cavalry riders astride Walers during World War I in 1914

INDONESIA
PAPUA NEW GUINEA
PACIFIC OCEAN
AUSTRALIA
Northern Territory
Queensland
Western Australia
South Australia
New South Wales
Victoria
INDIAN OCEAN
NEW ZEALAND
Tasmania

Brumby Range

Brumby range

An Australian Brumby

Since Brumbies aren't native, some people worry that they'll interfere with or harm Australia's natural ecosystems, but others want to protect the wild horses.

WHAT THE HECK IS A BRUMBY?

A Brumby is a wild Australian horse, the down-under equivalent of the American Mustang. Their ancestors arrived in 1788, with the British First Fleet, and eventually escaped to run wild. Most Brumbies are found in the arid areas of Australia, including Queensland and the Northern Territory.

AUSTRALIAN TACK

IF YOU THINK you have only two choices when it comes to tack—English or Western—you'd be mistaken. Australian-style tack is becoming increasingly popular around the world.

Australian saddles look a bit like the English saddles they were based on. The Aussies tinkered with the design, making it better suited to the rigors of the land down under. The result is a saddle that is very comfortable for both the rider and the horse. At an average of 15 pounds, it's lighter than a Western saddle. An Aussie saddle has stirrups that swing freely and a high pommel without a horn. The most noticeable feature are the poleys, which brace the rider's thighs and keep him or her in the saddle while the horse travels down steep slopes. Combined, all these practical features make the Australian saddle a favorite among competitive endurance riders.

The Thoroughbred: The World's Horse

Every October, excitement runs through the Thoroughbred world. It is time for the Breeder's Cup, the world championship of Thoroughbred racing. Countries from all over the world—Dubai, South Africa, Ireland, France, Great Britain, and the United States—send their best horses to compete in two days' worth of great racing. The event is held at a different racetrack, almost always in the United States, each year.

Although many breeds are found around the world, the Thoroughbred is truly the "world's horse." The breeding and racing of these horses has been a passion and a business for more than 400 years.

Today's Thoroughbred, no matter where it hails from, has its roots in England. There, selective breeding of native mares and imported stallions produced horses that were strong and fast—faster than any horse had ever been.

Horse and Rider

Thoroughbreds are natural athletes. These long-legged and muscular horses stand between 15 and 17 hands. The profile is straight and the neck is long. The most common Thoroughbred colors are bay, brown, chestnut, and gray. Roans and pintos are rare. In races, Thoroughbreds carry their riders, or jockeys.

A Thoroughbred racehorse

A bird's-eye view of the Churchill Downs racetrack in Louisville, Kentucky. This racetrack is the home of the Kentucky Derby, one of the most popular sporting events in the United States.

Most jockeys are small and light but amazingly strong and skilled. Jockeys usually weigh between 110 and 115 pounds. (Gross but true: to lower their weight, jockeys often force themselves to vomit. Some racetracks even have a special room for this activity, referred to as "flipping" in the racing world.)

Sometimes, particularly strong or successful horses are required to bear extra weight during a race. Additional weight takes the form of lead slabs placed in special pockets in the saddlecloth. Races can range from five furlongs (a furlong equals 220 yards, or an eighth of a mile) to 1.5 miles. Reaching speeds of up to 40 miles per hour, Thoroughbreds fly over the track at 60 feet per second.

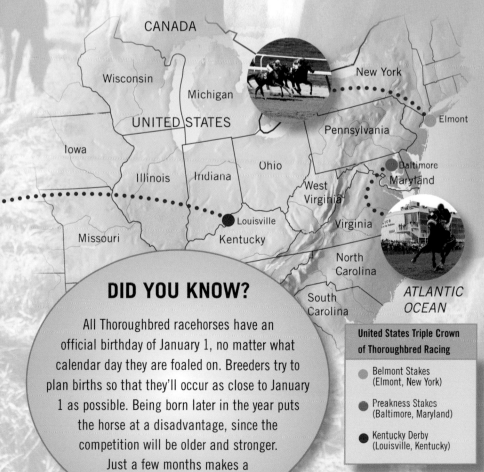

CANADA

Wisconsin

Michigan

New York

UNITED STATES

Elmont

Pennsylvania

Iowa

Ohio

Illinois   Indiana

West Virginia

Baltimore
Maryland

Louisville

Virginia

Missouri

Kentucky

North Carolina

DID YOU KNOW?

All Thoroughbred racehorses have an official birthday of January 1, no matter what calendar day they are foaled on. Breeders try to plan births so that they'll occur as close to January 1 as possible. Being born later in the year puts the horse at a disadvantage, since the competition will be older and stronger. Just a few months makes a big difference.

South Carolina

ATLANTIC OCEAN

United States Triple Crown of Thoroughbred Racing

- ● Belmont Stakes (Elmont, New York)
- ● Preakness Stakes (Baltimore, Maryland)
- ● Kentucky Derby (Louisville, Kentucky)

HORSES WITH A LOT OF HEART

ONE THING THAT all these great racehorses had in common—and what Thoroughbreds are known for—is heart. What's heart? It's a refusal to quit, even when the odds are stacked against you. Thoroughbreds know that heart makes all the difference.

Secretariat: In 1973, he won racing's Triple Crown. That means he took first pace in three big races—the Kentucky Derby, the Preakness, and the Belmont Stakes—a feat that hadn't been achieved since 1948. He did it in a big way, too, winning the last race by an amazing 31 lengths (a length is about 8 feet).

Ruffian: Born in 1972, this filly (a young female horse) burst onto the racing scene, either matching or beating the track record every time she ran.

Genuine Risk: She was one of only three fillies to ever win the Kentucky Derby (1980).

Seattle Slew: Four years after Secretariat won the Triple Crown, lightning struck again, in the form of a colt that had been so ungainly as a foal that he'd earned the nickname "Baby Huey," after a bumbling cartoon character.

Affirmed: In 1978, Affirmed won the Triple Crown, despite the efforts of another colt, Alydar. The pair provided thrills as they met time and again, but Affirmed affirmed his greatness, winning seven out of nine times.

Cigar: The winningest American horse of all time, this grandson of Seattle Slew tied the record for wins in a row (16), while winning almost $10 million.

Barbaro: After winning the 2006 Kentucky Derby, Barbaro seemed destined for Triple Crown greatness. Fate had other plans. He shattered his leg in the Preakness. For months, veterinarians struggled to save him, but bravery wasn't enough. In the end, his owners decided Barbaro had fought hard enough, and had him put to sleep.

New World of Wonders

You may not think of the eastern United States—home to cities like New York, Boston, and Washington, D.C.—as a hotbed of horse breeding, but more than 15 breeds of horses have been developed east of the Mississippi. One of those breeds is the Quarter Horse.

Although the Quarter Horse is strongly identified with the Wild West, it was first developed in Virginia in the 1600s. The English colonists there traded their imported horses with those of the members of the Chickasaw nation. The Chickasaw had gotten horses from the Spanish, who had settled in Florida in the mid-1500s. When mated together, the English and the Chickasaw steeds produced horses that were really fast for short distances.

What would you do with such a fast horse? Race it, of course! By the end of the century, Virginia races offered so much money that competitors began to arrive from other colonies. One of the most notable was Old Snipe, a horse owned by William Robinson of Rhode Island. When Virginia breeders added Old Snipe's bloodline to their horses, the Quarter Horse was born. Its name comes from running in quarter-mile races. Even now, the Quarter Horse is the fastest horse on the track for short-distance racing.

PONY PENNING DAY

EVER SEE a horse swim? How about a whole herd? How about a whole herd, swimming to support a volunteer fire department?

That's what the wild ponies that live on Assateague, a barrier island that runs along the Maryland and Virginia coasts do every July. The ponies on the Maryland side of the island belong to the federal government. On the Virginia side, the ponies are owned by the Chincoteague fire department. Every year, volunteer riders go to the island and round up the ponies. Then, the ponies swim across the channel between the islands and are herded through town. At the fairgrounds, some of the ponies are auctioned off, with proceeds benefiting the department. During this event, called Pony Penning Day, the ponies get routine veterinary checkups and vaccinations. Afterward, the remaining ponies swim back to Assateague.

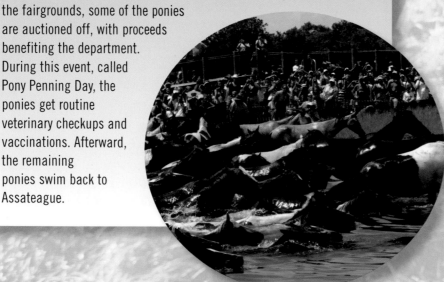

MORE BREEDS OF THE EASTERN UNITED STATES

Breed	Origin
American Walking pony	Georgia
Banker horse	North Carolina
Chickasaw	Florida
Chincoteague pony	Virginia
Florida Cracker	Southeast
Kentucky Mountain saddle horse	Eastern Kentucky
McCurdy Plantation horse	Alabama
Morab	New England
National Spotted saddle horse	Tennessee
Racking horse	Southeast
Rocky Mountain horse	Eastern Kentucky
Single-footing horse	Southeast

Standardbred horse,
Rhode Island

Morgan
horse,
Vermont

CANADA

Maine

Vermont New
Hampshire

Wisconsin   Michigan   Massachusetts
                        Boston
            New York   Rhode Island
                      Connecticut
                        New York

            Pennsylvania
                        Philadelphia

        Ohio   Baltimore
Illinois Indiana   West   Maryland
                   Virginia Virginia
        Kentucky

UNITED STATES
                   North
                   Carolina
      Tennessee
                South
                Carolina

                        ATLANTIC
            Atlanta   OCEAN

Mississippi   Georgia

   Alabama

                    Florida

Gulf of Mexico

Quarter Horse,
Virginia

Saddlebred
horses,
Kentucky

Go Figure!

A Vermont teacher gets the credit for one
Eastern breed. In 1791, Justin Morgan
received two horses as payment for a debt.
One was a strapping big gelding and the
other an undersized stallion named Figure.
Figure weighed barely 1,000 pounds and
stood less than 14 hands. Morgan sold the
gelding easily, but nobody wanted Figure—he
seemed too little. So Morgan rented the horse
to a neighboring farmer. That was when
everything changed. Figure did everything
the farmer asked, from hauling logs to
plowing fields, and never lost the sparkle in
his eye. After Figure pulled a giant log that
other horses had failed to budge, he became
famous. Today's Morgans still bear the stamp
of their remarkable forefather—they're just
bigger, ranging from 14.1 to 15.2 hands. And
like Figure (renamed Justin Morgan after his
owner died), they can do just about anything.

In the Wilds of the West

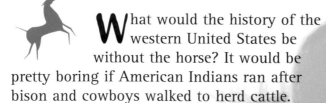

What would the history of the western United States be without the horse? It would be pretty boring if American Indians ran after bison and cowboys walked to herd cattle.

The horse changed the history of the American West. For instance, some American Indians had used dogs to pull a travois, a kind of sled made of two long poles. Some dog breeds are strong, but horses are stronger. And did you ever try to ride a dog? In the 1700s and 1800s, the horse carried settlers into the West and helped them herd cattle.

With so many horses, there were bound to be some runaways. The smartest, strongest ones managed to avoid being eaten by wolves, bears, coyotes, and mountain lions. They also found enough food and water to survive. They became a uniquely American horse, the Mustang.

Today, the Bureau of Land Management (BLM) oversees the Mustangs. The BLM runs a program that gives people a chance to adopt a wild horse. When gentled (tamed), Mustangs make excellent saddle horses and mounts for endurance races.

Some strains of Mustangs have had little contact with other horses, and so retain almost pure Spanish blood. Approximately 150 of this type, Pryor Mountain Mustangs, live on a preserve between Montana and Wyoming. Kiger Mustangs, found in eastern Oregon, look very much like the early Spanish horses; their heritage goes back to the Sorraia horses that Columbus's crew brought with them. Mustangs truly are living history.

MORE BREEDS OF THE WESTERN UNITED STATES

Breed	Origin
Cerbat	Arizona
Colorado Ranger	Colorado
International Striped Horse	Colorado
Missouri Fox Trotter	Missouri
Montana Traveler	Montana
Moyle horse	Idaho
National Show Horse	Arizona
North American spotted draft	Iowa
Pony of the Americas	Iowa
Sulphur horse	Utah
Tiger horse	Northwest
Wilber-Cruce Mission horse	Southern Arizona

MUSTANGS IN TROUBLE

For almost 200 years, the Mustangs roamed free. But eventually, ranchers began to resent the wild horses, which they thought competed with their cattle for grass. They shot the horses or hired men to round them up and kill them. In 1900, about two million Mustangs lived in the West. By 1970, fewer than 20,000 Mustangs survived.

Then came Velma Johnston, also known as Wild Horse Annie. Her tireless work brought the Mustangs' plight to the attention of the American people. As a result, in 1971 Congress passed a law protecting Mustangs and wild burros. The law called these animals "symbols of the historic and pioneer spirit of the American West."

Mustang horse and foal, Nevada

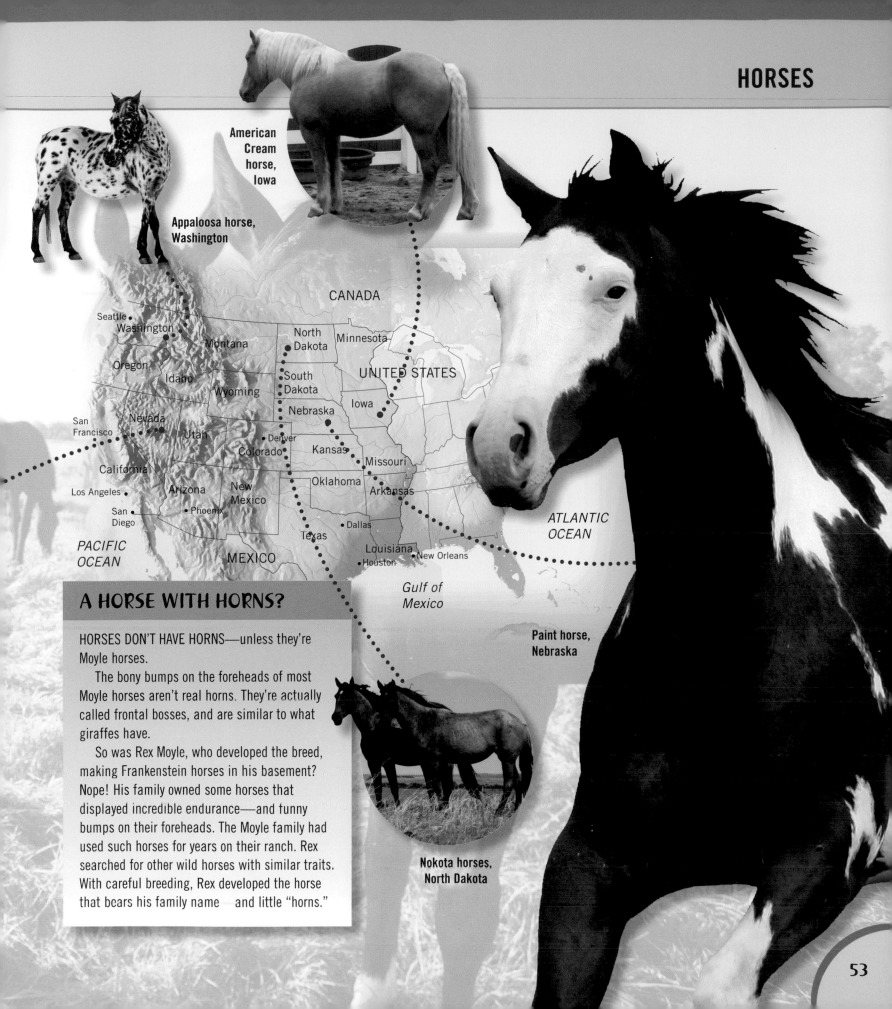

American Cream horse, Iowa

Appaloosa horse, Washington

CANADA

Seattle
Washington
Montana
North Dakota
Minnesota
Oregon
Idaho
South Dakota
UNITED STATES
Wyoming
Nebraska
Iowa
San Francisco
Nevada
Utah
Denver
Colorado
Kansas
Missouri
California
Arizona
New Mexico
Oklahoma
Arkansas
Los Angeles
San Diego
Phoenix
Dallas
Texas
Louisiana
New Orleans
Houston

ATLANTIC OCEAN

PACIFIC OCEAN

MEXICO

Gulf of Mexico

Paint horse, Nebraska

A HORSE WITH HORNS?

HORSES DON'T HAVE HORNS—unless they're Moyle horses.

The bony bumps on the foreheads of most Moyle horses aren't real horns. They're actually called frontal bosses, and are similar to what giraffes have.

So was Rex Moyle, who developed the breed, making Frankenstein horses in his basement? Nope! His family owned some horses that displayed incredible endurance—and funny bumps on their foreheads. The Moyle family had used such horses for years on their ranch. Rex searched for other wild horses with similar traits. With careful breeding, Rex developed the horse that bears his family name—and little "horns."

Nokota horses, North Dakota

American Indians and the Horse

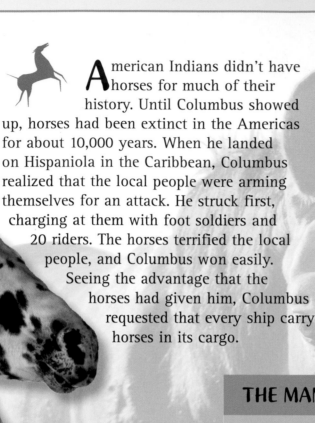

American Indians didn't have horses for much of their history. Until Columbus showed up, horses had been extinct in the Americas for about 10,000 years. When he landed on Hispaniola in the Caribbean, Columbus realized that the local people were arming themselves for an attack. He struck first, charging at them with foot soldiers and 20 riders. The horses terrified the local people, and Columbus won easily. Seeing the advantage that the horses had given him, Columbus requested that every ship carry horses in its cargo.

At the time, Spain's horses were among the finest in the world, and they flourished on the Caribbean islands, breeding well and growing strong. Later Spanish explorers bought these horses and took them to North America throughout the 1500s and 1600s.

Before the Spanish arrived, American Indians used dogs for pack animals. They hauled their belongings on travois (a sled made of poles) and stalked their prey on foot, just as their ancestors had.

The horse changed all that. The native peoples bought, stole, or caught horses that had strayed from the Spanish, French, and, later, American settlers—who bought, stole,

THE MANE FACTS: APPALOOSA

Height: 14.2–16.2 hh

Physical appearance: The head is small and well shaped. The eyes are large and the whites are visible. The neck is muscular and the withers moderately pronounced. Appaloosas traditionally have short, thin manes and tails, although modern breeders are creating thicker, longer ones. The hooves have vertical stripes. Most of all, Appaloosas have spots: either over their hindquarters (blanket, frost, or spotted blanket patterns) or all over (leopard, snowflake, or marble patterns).

Uses: Horse racing, Western events, eventing, foxhunting, and jumping

Cool stuff: Developed by the Nez Perce, the Appaloosa was almost destroyed when the tribe surrendered to the U.S. Army. Some tribe members escaped to Canada with their horses though, and other horses ran free or were hidden by local ranchers. Today, there are more than 15 million Appaloosas around the world!

or caught them right back. The horse gave American Indians unprecedented mobility and a huge advantage over any horseless enemies. Some nations, such as the Comanche and Kiowa, became fearsome mounted warriors. The Nez Perce gained fame for their spotted horses, the Appaloosa. The Chickasaw developed a breed of the same name that became important in developing the Quarter Horse. Within just a few generations, less than 100 years, some American Indian groups changed entirely from a settled existence to a nomadic one.

Today's American Indian horse preserves the qualities that the native peoples fostered in the horses of days of old.

Once American Indians owned horses, the animals rapidly became favorite subjects in native art. The horses themselves were also festooned with ornate and beautiful gear. Above, a chief adjusts his horse's decorated bridle.

DID YOU KNOW?

Horses have an excellent sense of smell, better than people but not quite as good as dogs. Their sense of smell is good enough to sniff out medicine mixed in with their food. One smell they don't like, apparently, is the smell of pigs.

American Indians quickly became proficient horse riders, using them to travel, hunt, and fight.

Horses of Iron

The Spanish and English weren't the only ones who decided to take horses to the New World. The French got in on the game, too. While the Spanish went to Florida and the English settled East Coast colonies, the French went to Canada.

Because their two countries were enemies, French and English settlers were forbidden to sell each other goods, trade horses, or have any dealings at all. So the French in Canada developed their horses without any influx of blood from their southern neighbors. The result was the Canadian horse. The breed produced trotters and pacers, making them good carriage horses, but they are flexible enough for farm work and riding. They earned the nickname the Little Iron Horse.

During the Seasons

The lives of the early Canadian horses were not easy. During the summer, they had to fend for themselves in the forests and woodlands. During the winter, they had no shelter, and were sometimes driven fast and far, left to shiver and wait for their owners to return. (Today, we call this animal abuse.) Despite this harsh treatment, the Canadian survived. It went on to influence many other breeds, passing on its courage and "iron horse" qualities to Morgans, Tennessee Walkers, Standardbreds, and others.

National Treasure

Canadian horses have been used so often for crossbreeding that the breed itself almost became extinct. Today, there are about 2,000 Canadians, mostly in Quebec. Almost always bay or black, Canadian horses have wavy manes and tails. They stand between 14.3 and 16.2 hands. They are recognized for their contribution to Canadian history: they are now the official national horse of Canada, a "national treasure."

The Calgary Stampede occurs annually in Alberta, Canada. Its outdoor rodeo competition is the largest in the world.

ARCTIC OCEAN

GREENLAND

Alaska

Yukon Territory

Nunavut

ATLANTIC OCEAN

Northwest Territories

Newfoundland

Hudson Bay

Alberta

British Colombia

Saskatchewan

Manitoba

CANADA

Quebec

Ontario

UNITED STATES

THE MANE FACTS: NEWFOUNDLAND PONY

Height: 12–14 hh

Physical appearance: The head is small and nicely shaped. The ears contain a lot of hair, which keeps them warm in winter and protects them from biting insects in the summer. The neck and shoulders are strong and muscular. The winter coat may be an entirely different color than the summer coat. In winter the mane lies on both sides of the neck, but in summer, it falls on only one side.

Uses: Historically, Canadians employed these hardy little ponies for farm work and transportation. During the twentieth century, after mechanical farm equipment replaced them, they were seen as a cheap source of meat. Today, the breed is used for riding and pulling carriages and sleighs.

Colors: Usually black, bay, brown or roan. White markings are rare.

Cool stuff: The Newfoundland's ancestors were probably British ponies, such as Dales and Fell ponies, brought over in the early 1600s.

THE MOUNTIES

The members of Canada's national police force, the Royal Canadian Mounted Police (RCMP), are instantly recognizable. They wear broad-brimmed Stetson hats and scarlet jackets. And what would a Mountie be without a horse?

Although most members of the RCMP don't ride anymore, the tradition of the Mounties lives on in the "Musical Ride." Carefully chosen officers ride nearly identical black horses that stand between 16 and 17.2 hands. The horses, however, are not Canadians; they are crosses of Thoroughbred, Trakehner, Hanoverian, and Anglo-Arab horses. During a performance, they execute precise drill maneuvers. The big black horses and their scarlet-coated riders keep history and Canadian pride alive.

Although the Mounties usually ride horses only in celebrations today, at one time their mounts served as important a role as their riders in keeping the peace throughout Canada.

Western Tack

Western tack looks very different from English tack. You've seen it—it's the stuff cowboys use. But in case you thought that a big horn makes riding Western easier than riding Eastern, well, pardner, you'd be wrong.

Today's Western saddles show their hardworking, cowpunching origins. The saddle horn—a useful handle to help you keep your grip in the saddle—once served as the anchor point for the cowboy's end of a rope, with a calf or a steer on the other end. The broad cantle provided a soft spot to land in case a cowpoke's horse sent him briefly airborne. The full stirrups made mounting and dismounting a snap.

The biggest difference between English and Western tack is how the saddle fastens on the horse. English saddles' girths run from the center of the saddle around the horse's barrel, and up to the other side. This centered arrangement is perfect for jumping fences. But a cowboy was less likely to jump a fence than he was to screech to a stop with a heavy bovine (cow or bull) at the end of his rope. A center-girth saddle can slip forward when a horse slams on the brakes. So, Western saddles have a two-point girth system instead: one near the front, and one near the rear. Only the front girth is cinched up tight.

The second one hangs about 2 inches from the horse's belly. The second girth works as a kind of insurance against saddle slippage.

Some Western saddles are real works of art. Saddle makers carve designs into the leather by hand (called "hand tooling"). They also add brilliant silver conchos (disc-shaped ornaments) and other silver decorations. Such saddles are shown off in parades, such as the Tournament of Roses. There, riders and horses decked out in their finest show the world what a Western saddle can really be!

Most riders, though, aren't worried about sudden stops or parade finery. They get along just fine with plainer saddles. Yet these saddles have the same distinctive features as their flashier cousins.

Western tack was developed to suit the needs of cowboys, responsible for herding cattle from horseback.

Cowboys use Western saddles to tame wild or unmanageable horses. The double-girth system protects both horse and rider.

DID YOU KNOW?

The Western saddle developed from the saddles the Spanish conquistadors used on their horses!

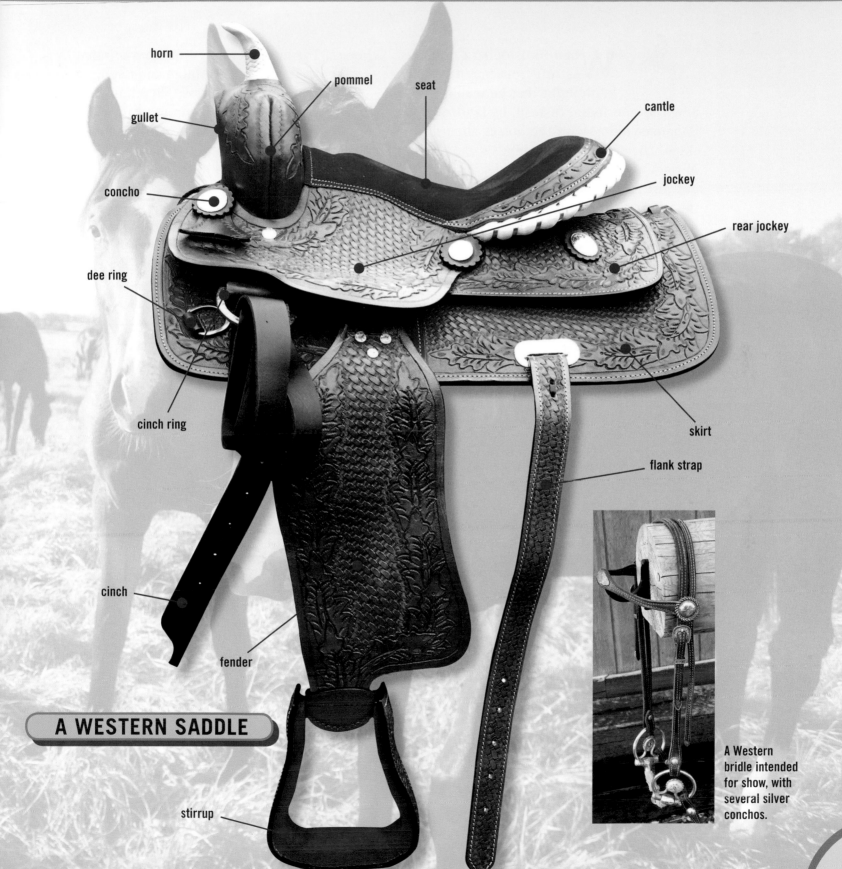

horn

pommel

seat

gullet

cantle

concho

jockey

rear jockey

dee ring

cinch ring

skirt

flank strap

cinch

fender

stirrup

A WESTERN SADDLE

A Western bridle intended for show, with several silver conchos.

Steeds of the Conquerors

When Christopher Columbus set off from Spain in 1492, he thought that he would find a new route to India. Instead, he landed in the Bahamas, along with the horses aboard his ships. The arrival of Columbus's expedition in the Caribbean was a historical event and not just for the obvious reason: it also marked the return of the horse to the New World, where it had evolved but had disappeared from 10,000 years earlier.

Horses Return to America

The horses that arrived with Columbus were unbelievably tough. Travel by ship was miserable for humans—and even worse for horses. The horses endured the journey tied on the deck, exposed to the blazing sun, seaspray, and raging storms. They hung in slings, which kept them from escaping, but also swung with the pitching of the ship. These horses were possibly Andalusians but may have been Sorraia horses, native to Portugal, or Jennets from Libya.

The human companions of the surviving horses quickly set up horse farms. The islands of the Caribbean became fine horse-breeding country. By 1509, breeding farms existed on Hispaniola, Jamaica, and Cuba. The horses produced on these island farms were beautiful animals, and they enabled the Spanish to conquer much of South and Central America. Without these farms, the Spanish conquistadors would have had to import their horses from Spain, and there just wouldn't have been enough horses to go around.

Diverse Horses

Today, the formerly Spanish lands in the Caribbean and Mexico are home to unique breeds of horses. Cuba produced the Cuban Trotter (from crossing Canadian horses with the Spanish horses), the Cuban Paso (a fine gaited saddle horse), the native Criollo, the Patibarcina (a type of Cuban Trotter with a bit of Andalusian thrown in), and the Cuban Pinto. Puerto Rico gave the world the Paso Fino, a small but beautiful breed that features an inborn four-beat gait. Mexico declared its official horse to be the recently developed Azteca, and the country also hosts the Galiceño, an old breed that was among the first horses in Mexico.

Spanish conquistadors (conquerors) rolled through South and Central America, thanks in part to their equine companions.

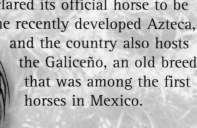

UNITED STATES

ATLANTIC OCEAN

Houston •

MEXICO •

Gulf of Mexico

• Guadalajara

PACIFIC OCEAN

BELIZE

GUATEMALA

HONDURAS

NICARAGUA

COSTA RICA

PANAMA

COLOMBIA

• Havana

CUBA

Santo
Domingo

PUERTO
RICO

DOMINICAN
REPUBLIC

Caribbean Sea

VENEZUELA

Paso Fino,
Puerto Rico

Azteca, Mexico

THE MANE FACTS: AZTECA

Height: 14.3–16 hh (mares), 15–16.1 hh (stallions)

Physical appearance: The profile is straight or slightly convex, with large eyes. The withers are high and lead into a short, straight back.

Uses: Riding, including dressage, pleasure, roping, cutting, even bullfighting

Colors: Gray is most common, but most colors are permitted, except for pinto and spotted.

Cool stuff: The Azteca is a relatively new breed. Efforts to create a uniquely Mexican breed started in 1972 by breeding Andalusians, Criollos, and Quarter Horses. No Azteca can be more than three-quarters of one of these foundation breeds. About 15,000 Aztecas exist today.

A beach on a tropical island is a nice place to visit, but not necessarily a great place to live—especially if you're a horse.

ISLANDS MAKE FOR LITTLE HORSES

Life on an island isn't all lounging on the beach. For animals and plants, islands can be tough environments indeed, with limited sources of food and water, little shelter, and unpredictable weather.

Because life on islands is hard, the creatures that live on them are usually smaller than their relatives on the mainland. Scientists have found that when island-dwelling horses are moved off the island, they often grow larger, reaching the same size as horses that have lived on the mainland their whole lives.

The Long Riders

Would you ride a horse from Argentina to the United States? Chances are, you answered, "No way!" How about if we sweeten the deal, and allow you to ride two horses—barely tamed geldings that are 15 and 16 years old?

Oh, and let's say you don't really know much about horses. If Aimé Tschiffely had known a lot about horses, he probably wouldn't have made his historic ride of more than 10,000 miles. But he knew history, and he wanted to prove that the Criollo, a South American breed descended from the horses of the conquistadors, was the toughest horse in the world. So, in 1925, he set out on a journey from Buenos Aires, Argentina, to Washington, D.C., in the United States.

Tschiffely was an unlikely adventurer. He had grown up in Switzerland and lived in England before going to Argentina to teach. Most people considered him absolutely nuts—especially people who knew anything about horses. But a lot of people did a lot of crazy things in the 1920s.

For the trip he took a 15-year-old buckskin named Gato ("Cat") and a 16-year-old pinto named Mancha ("Spotty"). Mancha wouldn't let anybody but Tschiffely ride him. Gato was a little nicer. Not only did the horses display less than charming temperaments, the horses were also homely. "As far removed

THE MANE FACTS: MANGALARGA MARCHADOR

Height: 14.3–15.2 hh

Physical appearance: Profile is straight, not dished, with a large forehead tapering to a fine muzzle. Ear tips turn inward, though not as pronounced as in the Marwari of India; its muscular arched neck is covered with a fine mane. Legs are long with short cannon bones.

Qualities: Gentle and easy to handle, but full of brio, or fire; a spirited bearing

Uses: Endurance and pleasure riding, as well as ranch work

Colors: Bay, chestnut, and gray are most popular.

Cool stuff: A true marcher, this breed has a special, super-smooth gait called the *marcha*, in which the horse keeps three legs on the ground at once. This is the national horse of Brazil, which houses more than a quarter of a million Marchadors. The first part of the name comes from the name of the *hacienda* (a ranch) that first promoted the breed.

Mangalarga
Marchador horse,
Brazil

Mangalarga Paulista horse, Brazil

. . . from a first-class English hunter as the North Pole from the South," Tschiffely wrote, describing them.

Yet Mancha, Gato, and Tschiffely survived storms, arid wastelands, mosquitoes, no food or water, sheer cliffs, and even a near miss with a car. Three years after leaving Argentina, U.S. president Calvin Coolidge welcomed them to the White House. Together, Tschiffely, Gato, and Mancha had proved to the world that the Criollo was an endurance horse without equal.

Gato and Mancha lived long lives after their adventure. Gato died in 1944 and Mancha in 1947, both over the age of 30. Tschiffely wrote several books about the trip, and went on to inspire generations of "long riders."

Llañero horse, Venezuela

Chilean horses, Chile

MORE BREEDS OF SOUTH AMERICA

Breed	Origin
Argentine polo pony	Argentina
Brazilian sport horse	Brazil
Campiero	Brazil
Campolina	Brazil
Chilote	Chile
Chola	Peru
Colombian saddle horse	Colombia
Costa Rican saddle horse	Costa Rica
Marajoara	Brazil
Northeastern	Brazil
Pantaniero	Brazil
Petiso Argentino	Argentina
Piquira pony	Brazil
Trote en Gallope	Colombia

VENEZUELA
COLOMBIA
ECUADOR
SOUTH AMERICA
PERU
BRAZIL
BOLIVIA
PARAGUAY
CHILE
ATLANTIC OCEAN
PACIFIC OCEAN
ARGENTINA
URUGUAY
Buenos Aires

Criollo horse, Argentina

Falabella miniature horse, Argentina

Wild Horses

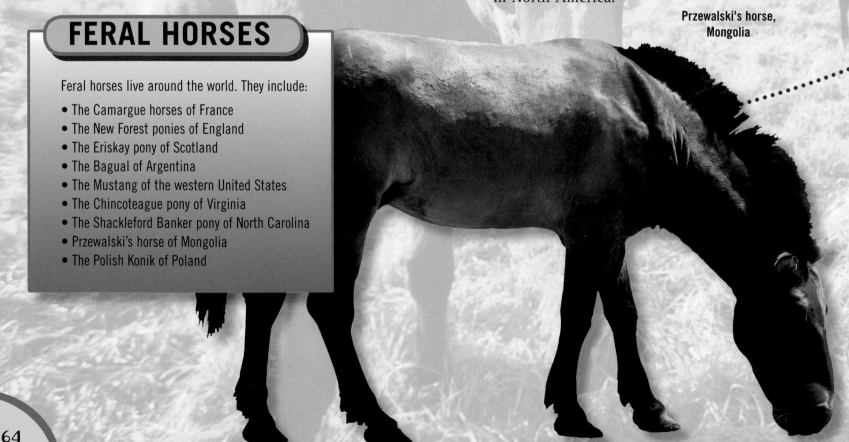

What does "wild" mean? A wild animal is one that has never been tamed or bred in captivity by human beings. Although there are groups of horses that live without human care and feeding, the correct term for them is *feral*. A feral animal is one that used to be tame but escaped and adjusted to living on its own. Governments treat feral animals differently than truly wild animals. That is, they usually don't give them the same degree of protection. Some people look at the American West's wild horses as feral invaders, creatures that compete with native wild species for food and water, and argue that the horses shouldn't be protected.

There is only one real wild horse: Przewalski's horse. This stocky, short-legged horse used to be found from Germany to China. Przewalski's horse went extinct in the wild because of hunting and habitat destruction (a small population remained in captivity). About 400 of them have been reintroduced into the wild.

Another wild horse, the tarpan, looked very similar to Przewalski's horse but lived in a different area, from France through Russia. The last tarpan died in 1876, but, during the 1930s, German scientists used selective breeding to "re-create" the tarpan. They used Icelandic horses, Gotland ponies, Polish primitive horses, and Polish Koniks, plus a bit of Przewalski's horse, to develop a modern-day version of the tarpan. Today, about 100 of these genetic revivals exist, most of them in North America.

A herd of Polish Koniks

Przewalski's horse, Mongolia

FERAL HORSES

Feral horses live around the world. They include:

- The Camargue horses of France
- The New Forest ponies of England
- The Eriskay pony of Scotland
- The Bagual of Argentina
- The Mustang of the western United States
- The Chincoteague pony of Virginia
- The Shackleford Banker pony of North Carolina
- Przewalski's horse of Mongolia
- The Polish Konik of Poland

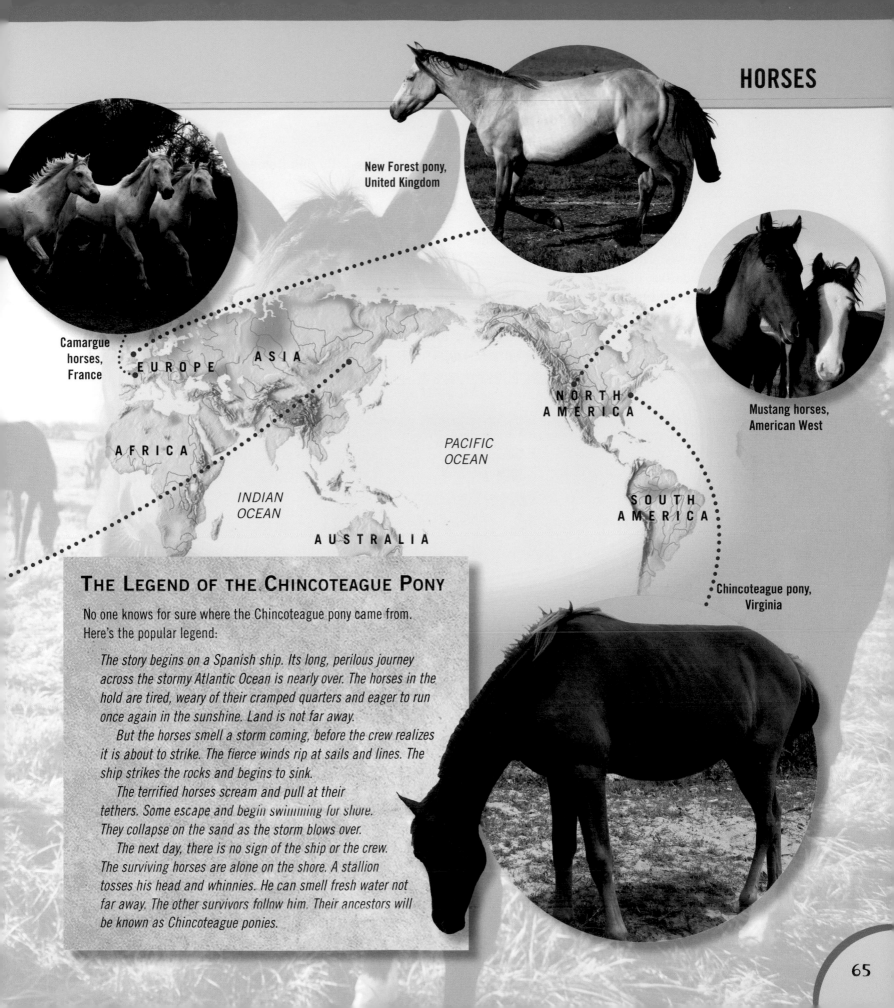

New Forest pony,
United Kingdom

Camargue
horses,
France

EUROPE   ASIA

AFRICA

INDIAN
OCEAN

PACIFIC
OCEAN

AUSTRALIA

NORTH
AMERICA

SOUTH
AMERICA

Mustang horses,
American West

Chincoteague pony,
Virginia

THE LEGEND OF THE CHINCOTEAGUE PONY

No one knows for sure where the Chincoteague pony came from.
Here's the popular legend:

*The story begins on a Spanish ship. Its long, perilous journey
across the stormy Atlantic Ocean is nearly over. The horses in the
hold are tired, weary of their cramped quarters and eager to run
once again in the sunshine. Land is not far away.*

*But the horses smell a storm coming, before the crew realizes
it is about to strike. The fierce winds rip at sails and lines. The
ship strikes the rocks and begins to sink.*

*The terrified horses scream and pull at their
tethers. Some escape and begin swimming for shore.
They collapse on the sand as the storm blows over.*

*The next day, there is no sign of the ship or the crew.
The surviving horses are alone on the shore. A stallion
tosses his head and whinnies. He can smell fresh water not
far away. The other survivors follow him. Their ancestors will
be known as Chincoteague ponies.*

The Horse's Relatives

Who would a horse invite to a family reunion? It turns out that the horse has some pretty interesting, wild relatives.

They're all members of the same genus, *Equus*. The horse's scientific name is *Equus caballus*, or just *E. caballus*. That name covers everything from the fastest Thoroughbred to the mightiest Shire to the stocky little Przewalski's horse. Even though they look vastly different, they're all horses. The other *Equus* family members are the asses and the zebras.

The Wild and Domestic Ass

The donkey is actually just one of the species of asses. Asses have loud, braying calls and longer ears than their horse cousins. Also known as the African wild ass, the donkey goes by the scientific name *E. asinus*. After originating in Africa, the donkey was domesticated about 6,000 years ago to help carry stuff, including people. Surefooted, small, and intelligent, the donkey is now found around the world.

Endangered in Asia

The onager is the Asiatic wild ass, *E. hemionus*. Although it looks a lot like a donkey, its ears, mane, and tail are shorter, and its hooves are broader. Originally, the onager lived in the desert and dry steppes of Asia, from India through the Ukraine. The onager is an endangered species, with only about 600 onagers in the wild. And their numbers are still falling.

Warm in the Mountains

The kiang, *E. kiang*, lives in Tibet, grazing on the mountain steppes as high up as 16,000 feet. To stay warm, it grows a long, thick winter coat. The kiang is the largest of the wild asses.

Wild Asses

onager range

kiang range

EUROPE

ASIA

PACIFIC OCEAN

Kiangs live in groups. They defend themselves by kicking with their powerful legs.

In ancient times, people harnessed onagers, such as this one at right, just like they did donkeys. Today, their wild descendants must fight to survive habitat loss and hunting.

Stripes by Design

The zebras are the showiest members of the horse family, but they can be pretty cranky, and they can't be domesticated. There are three surviving species: *E. zebra*, the mountain zebra; *E. grevyi*, Grevy's zebra, and *E. quagga*, the plains zebra (also known as Burchell's zebra). All zebras live in Africa. Are they all identical? Nope! Each zebra has a unique pattern of stripes, and the pattern differs among the species, too.

Zebras face danger from predators, especially lions. You'd think their stripes would make zebras very noticeable to lions, but that's not the case. When in a herd, any individual zebra is actually harder for a predator to make out. The striped pattern breaks up the body outlines and makes it hard for lions to see where one zebra ends and the next begins. A lion usually tries to split the difference and misses both zebras.

AFRICA

ATLANTIC OCEAN

INDIAN OCEAN

World of Zebras

zebra range

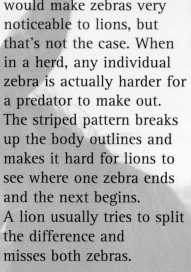

THE QUAGGA

THE QUAGGA LOOKED like an unfinished zebra. Striped at the front, it faded to a plain whitish color at the rear. Unfortunately, the quagga is extinct. It was hunted out of existence, with hunters in South Africa shooting the last wild one in 1878. The last quagga in captivity lasted until 1883, when it died on August 12 in the Amsterdam Zoo.

Scientists have discovered that the quagga was actually a subspecies of Burchell's zebra, just with fewer, fainter stripes. To make up for the extinction, a selective breeding program is underway in South Africa to "re-create" the quagga. So far, the project has succeeded in making zebras with fewer and fewer stripes. Henry, a foal born in 2005, is the most "quagga-like" foal produced so far.

DEADLY—ZEBRAS?

More zookeepers are injured or killed by zebras than by any other zoo animal. See, we told you they were cranky!

Find Out More

Words to Know

bit. The metal or rubber mouthpiece on the bridle that the reins attach to

blaze. A wide white stripe down a horse's face

bloodline. The ancestors of a horse

breed. A group of animals within a species that was selectively bred to produce certain characteristics

bridle. A piece of tack that is worn on the horse's head and allows the rider to control the horse

cold-blooded. A draft or heavyset horse

colt. A young male horse, usually less than four years old

conformation. The structure of a horse's body, particularly when compared with the written ideal for its breed

dam. A horse's mother

dressage. An equestrian event that requires horse and rider to perform a complex series of movements without the noticeable use of signals

endurance riding. Racing cross-country

eventing. A three- or four-day competition that tests the ability of horse and rider to complete a cross-country jumping course, a show-jumping course, and a dressage competition

evolution. The series of changes that organisms undergo as they adapt to the changing demands of their environment

feathering. Long hairs on a horse's lower legs, such as in the Shire and Clydesdale

feral. A formerly domesticated animal that has returned to a wild state

filly. A young female horse, usually less than four years old

foal. A baby horse

forelock. Hair that extends from between the ears and over the face

fossil. Bones that have become rock or impressions of living organisms left in rock

fossil record. A series of fossils that depict how an organism has changed during its evolution

foundation sire. A stallion who is considered the founder of a breed. For some breeds, all members can trace their descent from a single foundation sire.

frog. The soft part on the underside of a horse's hoof

gaited. A horse that has additional gaits, beyond the basic walk, trot, and canter

gelding. A male horse that has had its testicles removed

genus. A term biologists use in ranking relationships among organisms.

girth. The measure of a horse around under the belly. Also, a strap of leather or fabric used to hold a saddle in place on a horse's back

harness. A device used to hitch a horse to a carriage, wagon, or other vehicle

high-spirited. Lively in behavior, as compared to a horse that is more calm or docile

hock. The large joint in a horse's hind leg, above the cannon bone

hot-blooded. A type of horse that is highly spirited, particularly the Arabian and the Thoroughbred

mare. An adult female horse

pedigree. A listing of a horse's ancestors

pleasure riding. Riding a horse for enjoyment; pleasure classes in horse shows are judged largely on how much of a "pleasure" the horse appears to be to ride.

quarters. The horse's rear end

saddle. A seat for a rider placed on a horse's back and fastened around its belly

saddle horse. A horse ideal for riding

sire. A horse's father

sock. A white mark extending from the horse's hoof halfway up to its knee or hock

species. A group of living things capable of producing offspring

stallion. An adult male horse

stirrup. The part of a saddle that holds the rider's foot

stocking. A white marking extending from the horse's hoof to its knee on the foreleg or the hock on the hind leg

warm-blooded. A breed that has resulted from crossing Arabians or Thoroughbreds (hot-blooded breeds) with a more docile and heavily built cold-blooded breed

way of going. The manner in which a horse moves

withers. The point at which the neck meets the back

Books to Read

Dutson, Judith. *Storey's Illustrated Guide of 96 Horse Breeds of North America*. North Adams, MA: Storey Publishing, 2005.

Hendricks, Bonnie. *International Encyclopedia of Horse Breeds*. Norman, OK: University of Oklahoma Press, 2007.

Henry, Marguerite. *Album of Horses*. New York: Aladdin Paperbacks, 1993.

Meltzer, Milton. *Hold Your Horses! A Feedbag Full of Facts and Fables*. New York: Harper-Collins, 1995.

Peterson, Cris. *Horsepower: The Wonder of Draft Horses*. Honesdale, PA: Boyds Mills Press, 1997.

Ransford, Sandy. *The Kingfisher Illustrated Horse and Pony Encyclopedia*. Boston: Kingfisher Books, 2004.

Yue, Charlotte and David Yue. *Armor*. Boston: Houghton Mifflin, 1994.

Web Sites to See

Equiworld
www.equiworld.net/uk

"Horse Evolution Followed Twisty Trail"
www.nationalgeographic.com/news/2005/03/0317_050317_horseevolution.html

Oklahoma State University
www.ansi/okstate/breeds/horses

Index

knight, 30, 32, 33, 38, 39
Konik horse, 33, 64

L

Lascaux cave, 21
La Perch horse, 38
levade, 34
Lipizzaner horse, 25, 34
Llañero horse, 63
Lusitano horse, 24

M

Mangalarga Marchador, 24, 62
Mangalarga Paulista, 63
Marwari horse, 25, 44, 45, 62
Merychippus, 18, 19
Mesohippus, 18, 19
Michelangelo, 21
Middle Ages, 21, 30, 32, 37, 38
miniature horse, 13
Misaki horse, 44
Mongolian horse, 44
Moors, 28, 33
Morgan horse, 51, 56
Morgan, Justin, 51
Moyle horse, 53

Moyle, Rex, 53
Mustang, 47, 52, 65

N

Namib Desert horse, 29
Nejd horse, 27
Newfoundland pony, 57
New Forest pony, 37, 65

Nez Perce, 54, 55
Nokota horse, 53
Nooitgedacht pony, 25, 29

O

Oligocene epoch, 18
onager, 66
Orohippus, 18

P

Paint horse, 53
Paleolithic age, 21
Parthenon, the, 21
Paso Fino, 29, 60, 61
Patibarcina horse, 60
Patton, George, 35
Percheron horse, 38
Peruvian Paso, 16
Philip II of Macedon, 31
Pleistocene epoch, 20
Pliocene epoch, 18, 19
Pliohippus, 19
Podjahsky, Alois, 35
Polish primitive horse, 64
polo pony, 17
Pony Penning Day, 50
Poseidon, 21
Preakness Stakes, 49
Pryor Mountain Mustang, 52
Przewalski's horse, 64, 66

Q

quagga, 67
Quarter Horse, 24, 29, 46, 50, 51, 61

R

Rathore people, 45
Robinson, William, 50
Royal Canadian Mounted Police, 57

S

Saddlebred horse, 43, 51
Selle Français, 12
Shetland pony, 17, 36, 37
Shire horse, 10, 36, 37, 38, 66
show saddle, 42
Sorraia horse, 52, 60
Spanish Barb, 29
Spanish Riding School, 34, 35
Standardbred horse, 51, 56
Suffolk horse, 36

T

tarpan, 64
Tennessee Walker, 43, 56
Thoroughbred horse, 12, 46, 48, 49, 57, 66
Tibetan pony, 44
Tournament of Roses, 58
Trakehner horse, 12, 57
Triple Crown, 49
Tschiffely, Aimé, 62
Turk horse, 26

U

unicorn, 21

W

Waler horse, 46
Welsh mountain pony, 17
Welsh pony, 17, 37, 46
Western bridle, 59
Western saddle, 47, 58
Western tack, 47, 58
World War I, 33, 46
World War II, 28, 30, 35

X

Xenophon, 20

Y

Yunnan horse, 44

Z

zebra, 16, 20, 66, 67
  Burchell's, 67
  Grevy's, 67

Credits